MODERN PERSPECTIVE OF PRINCIPLES OF KRIYA SHARIR

A CONCEPTUAL UNDERSTANDING

DR.SHUBHA KAUSHAL
DR.MANJU SHARMA

Title: MODERN PERSPECTIVE OF PRINCIPLES OF KRIYA SHARIR :A CONCEPTUAL UNDERSTANDING.
Language: English
Character set encoding: UTF-8

First published by

An Imprint of BlueRose Publishers

Head Office: B-6, 2nd Floor,
ABL Workspaces, Block B, Sector 4,
Noida, Uttar Pradesh 201301
M: +91-8882 898 898

BlueRose ONE .com
Stories Matter
DIY

In the fond memory of our beloved brother

SHAHEED CAPT.ROHIT KAUSHAL

We do hope that the students and scholars of ayurveda will surely benefit from the contents contained in this book.

ACKNOWLEDGEMENTS

We are deeply indebted to God for being a guiding spirit throughout the journey of this effort.The book would not have been possible without using the vast insightful knowledge from the following sources :-

Charak samhita

Sushrut samhita

Ashtang sangrah

Ashtang hridey

Ayurvedic sharir kriya vigyan -Shiv Kumar Gaur

Sharir kriya vigyan -vd.Ranjit Rai Desai

Basic Principles of kriya Sharir-Dr.Srikant Kumar Panda

Sharir Kriya Vigyan-Dr. Sunil Yadav ,Prof. Jairam Yadav

www.wjpmr.com

https:www.easyayurveda.com

www.ayurlog.com

www.ncbi.nih.gov

Human Physiology in Ayurveda-Dr.Kishor Patwardhan

Human Physiology-CC Chatterjee

Sharir Kriya Vigyanm-Vd.Shivcharan Dhyani.

Prakrit Agni Vigyan-Niranjan Dev Ayurvedalankar

Prakrit Dosha Vigyan-Niranjan Dev Ayurvedalankar

Digestion evam Metabolism in Ayurved-C.Dwarkanath

www.research gate.com

thanks to google for images.

ACKNOWLEDGEMENTS

God has been there at every step of the way a sincere gratitude to HIM for HIS ever unconditional blessings.

PREFACE

PREFACE

When a student after studying science with modern aspects suddenly gets admission in Ayurveda - he is confused and a bit out of the place. For sure they know they are future doctors but the difference of Ayurvedic philosophies and Modern description of physiology of human body , its diseases, pathology somewhere doesn't match and synchronises to their already mind setup, and the outcome is a half-hearted acceptance to the pathy and an incomplete clarity of it.

The purpose of this book is not to boast Kriya Sharir Just because one of the authors is part and parcel of this subject from last twenty three years. The reason to introduce this book is the fact that Students normally do not do complete justice to this subject. Whereas it's the foundation subject of Ayurvedic concepts and theories.

Ayurveda is the holistic science that seeks to treat and integrate body, mind and spirit using a comprehensive holistic approach especially by emphasizing diet, herbal remedies, exercise, meditation, breathing, and physical therapy. It's a PCHS i.e Person Centered Healing System, which believes in healthy life style, health promotion and sustenance, disease prevention, diagnosis and treatment. There is absolutely no harm in accepting modern approach of science but one should learn to balance the cultural differences.

This book aims to bring into limelight the age old basic principles of Ayurveda in modern perspective, with a hope that this would help the budding scholars, researchers gain deeper perspicuity of traditional systems of medicine, facilitate strengthening of the commonalities and overcome the challenges towards their Ayurvedic system understanding.

DR.Shubha Kaushal

DR.Manju Sharma

KURUKSHETRA.

(Authors)

10TH JULY 2022.

PROLOGUE

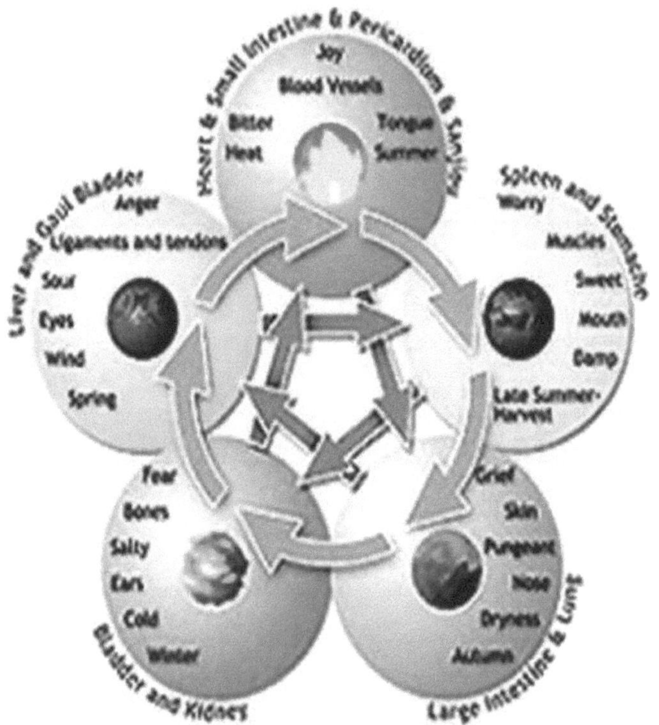

Concepts of Ayurveda

AYURVED

Throughout the world there are innumerable treatment systems operating some traditional and some generalised globally accepted ones. Even in India, there are such traditional systems i.e- AYUSH – Ayurved , Yoga,

Unani, Sidha, Homeopathy. But the most dominant of the six is Ayurveda- in India as well as globally. The most accepted , one is - this. Since it has a dynamic, diverse aspects of managing health, well being and unbroken Knowledge tradition. Contemporary Ayurveda is formalized and institutionalised on aspects such as education, clinical approaches, pharmacopia, manufacturing, Researches etc. The Ayurvedic concepts and theories are quite generic and simple yet consistent efforts to scientifically interpret and utilize Ayurvedic knowledge through the eyes of modern science is the need of the hour. Although various research institutes and Postgraduate institutes of Ayurveda along with many manufacturing companies is working constantly, and improvising methods and techniques to establish this renowned old traditional system of healing at par to the modern science concepts and theories.

For true exploration and validation of Ayurveda in all aspects, scientific inputs should conform to Ayurveda as basic principles and philosophy. The lack of the understanding of the differences and similarities between the theoretical doctrines of these systems is the major hurdle towards their convergence .

Ayurveda is the trademark of all pathies. In fact we can proudly say that almost all the pathies have originated one way or the other through this pathy only. It's the foundation and milestone of all kinds of treatments being the system originated from Brahma and the knowledge of this system is immortal being the inseparable part of the four vedas of Hindu mythology. [Yajur Veda, Saam Veda, Rig Veda, Atharva Veda] It's narrated in the history of origin of Ayurveda that Brahma the creator of the universe showered his blessing in the form of knowledge to Indra who showered it to Atreya. Agnivesh compiled the knowledge from Vedas which was edited by CHARAK as Charak Samhita. Charak Samhita describes the medicinal part of Ayurvedic treatment and diagnosis whereas the "SushrutSamhita covers the surgical aspects of diseases.Both these legendary compilations are from years and till date the base of understanding and implementing Ayurvedic approach.

Ayurveda -Ayu -age, veda-an ocean of knowledge with ancient origin must be the most accepted system of providing health but the practical inexperiences associated with this holistic science is one the major reason that despite being the oldest and the best its still waiting for its crown ceremony.

Although in todays world of pomp and show and moderanisation of everything.when its in concern of ayurveda we can proudly say - "old is Gold " When it's about healing physically or mentally. Ayurveda acharyas have acknowledged and documented various information and theories through their insight perception. Since we are living in an era of platinum, it's time for the Golden Ayurved to be polished with the logical reasoning to make it the platinum of todays medical stream. Although the oldest yet the best with an approach of keeping the body in balance not only at physical level but also at mental level .This science is Lagging behind and has not still found it's due due to lack of scientific evidence in global sector with many limited research means and methodology, But a lot of work is been done by pioneer institutes of Ayurveda to overcome this Lacuna. Hopefully in a very near future this veda will have Global acceptance as the best healing system.

CONTENTS

1. KRIYA SHARIR

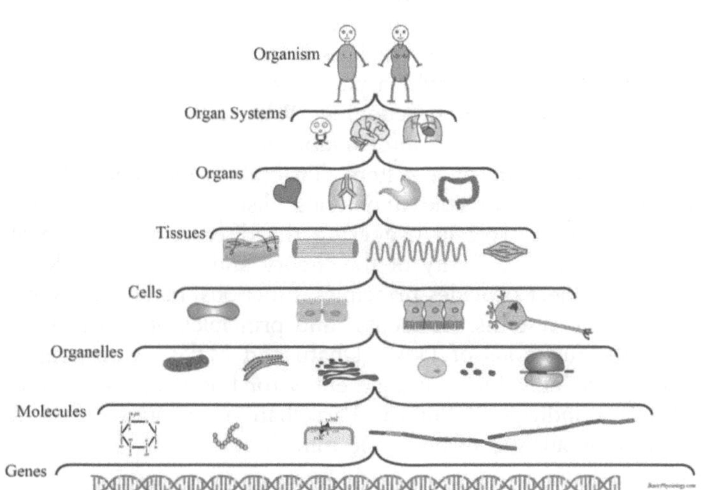

KRIYA SHARIR

Kriyasharir is made from two words : kriya (action)

and

sharir (body).

It's one of the most important and the basic subject of Ayurvedic medical science. As it not only spreads light on the normal prakritik functions of different systems of the human body but this subject also forms the root/base of the theory of Ayurveda around which the rest of the subjects and treatments of Ayurveda depends upon.

Since it's the base, the fundamental milestone of learning and understanding Ayurveda, its concepts and the practical implication of its theories is must to be well known to every Ayurvedist. This subject is grounded in the first year of the graduation period of Ayurveda. Most of the students at the initial stage don't realise the importance of this subject and with the result the subsequent subjects and concepts become a difficult thing to grab.

The whole focus of this subject revolves around the normal functioning patterns of each and every system. Thorough study of each system gives the clear picture of what all goes on in a system, who all are responsible for the functioning, which Dosha, which dhatu or mala is in imbalanced state ,which hormones, which enzymes, which part of the nervous system plays chief role in physiological functioning. What functions are taken care of by which system, this information helps us to recognise the abnormality in any part of a system. To build a diagnosis of the system involved, the possible underlying disease, the factors that must have played a role in triggering the disease, answers to all these queries lie in the clarity of the theory and concepts of Kriya Sharir as this subject provides principles, functions, mechanisms and actions of bodily systems. Concepts and principles of Sharir Kriya deals with the functions of Dosh, Dhatu and Malas. According to Ayurveda, every individual is unique entity for knowing this uniqueness of every individual 'Prakriti Parikshan' is essential. 'Prakriti Parikshan' is the analysis of body and mind.

Kriya Sharir vigyan deals with the basic concepts, knowledge and aaplicability of tridosha-Vata ,Pitta, Kapha as tridosha siddhant, sapta dhatu siddhant, malas siddhant, prakriti siddhant. Be it any disease it can not be understood unless dosha-dhatu-mala equation in respect to each other and their levels are properly assessed.

" Dosha dhatu mala moolam hee shariram"

The basic theory of ayurveda along with its kriya sharir aspect revolves around the three entities .And its believed that whatsoever good or bad happens inside the body its because of them and actually in them. Balance of the trio is health....any imbalance amongst any of them imbalances the whole bodily functions and in case this imbalance persists for long it ends up in a diseased condition .

Since its the basic principle of Ayurveda the proper knowledge of it in depth is a must to understand the kriya of body its very much essential to understand the normal and abnormal functionings of these entities.

1. DOSHA

(VATA, PITTA, KAPHA - TRIDOSHA)

2 .DHATU

(Seven in Number Rasa, Rakta, Mamsa, Meda, Asthi, Majja, Shukra)

3 . MALA

[Mutra (Urine) , Purish (Faeces), Swed (Sweat)]

As the word mool means root. Just if the roots are cut, the tree can no longer survive so is the role of these three entities in maintaining of life in a body. So the dynamic balanced state of these three [Bionergies, Tissues & wastes] defines a healthy person. Any inequilibrium in any of these three or from any of these three calls for diseased triggering factor or even a disease. That's why Ayurved acharyas have mentioned them as the base, fundament foundation of healthy state.

2. PANCHMAHABHUT

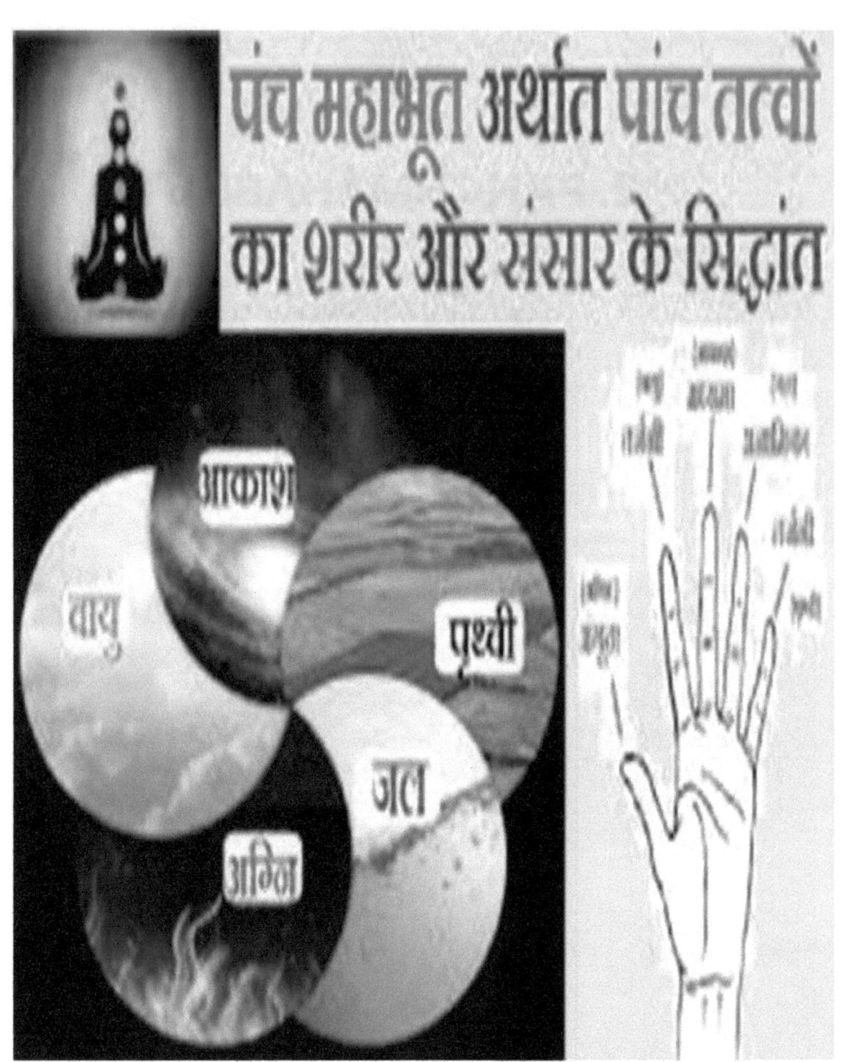
पंच महाभूत अर्थात पांच तत्वों
का शरीर और संसार के सिद्धांत
आकाश
वायु
पृथ्वी
जल
अग्नि

PANCHMAHABHOOT THEORY

नजायतेअन्यतोयक्तुयस्मात्अन्यतेत्प्रजायतेसगुणानांउपादानंतद्भूतम्कथ्यते

To understand Panchmahabhuta we first need to understand *Bhuta.*

Bhuta means the one who have their own origin; they cannot be created from anything. They are the basic elements through which the five elements are formed. Bhuta is also known as Tanmatra, from these bhutas Panchmahabhuta originate.

महान्तिभूतानिमहाभूतानि

Bhuta are Karan Dravye (causal factor) and ever existing (Nitya). At the time of Evolution/SristhiRachna / creation of universe life element (Purusha) and Nature (Prakriti with 3 Gunas)(सत्व + रंज + तम) in balanced state will get united in a cosmic union from this union Mahan is created Mahan gives rise to Ahankaar (cosmic Intelligence) [cosmic Egoism] from which five Tanmatras originate

First level- Evolution of Panchtanmatra (subtle elements)

Second level - Bhutantranupravesha (Imitative Pervasion)

Third level - Panchikaran (Reciprocal Pervasion)

As we know everything in this universe is made up of Panchmahabhuta there is a fundamental harmony. At the macrocosm level and microcosm level as our body is a very minute image of the universe.

Ayurveda- the ancient science of centuries, its basic foundation is –Panchmahabhoot. They are the minutest elements. It is believed that every matter be it living or non living is made up of five elements and these matters differ from each other due to the difference in the proportion of these five elements in each matter. These five elements are Earth (Prithvi), Water (Jal), Fire (Agni/Tej), AIR (Vayu), Space/Ether (Akash) they are collectively termed as Panchmahabhoot.

Mahabhoot	Main sense attribute	Main prope
AKASH/ SPACE/ETHER	SHABDA	APRATIGH
AIR/VAYU	SHABDA + SPARSHA	CHALATW
FIRE/AGNI	SHABDA+SPARSHAT ROOP	USHNATW
WATER/JAL	SHABDAT SPARSHA+ ROOP + RASA	DRAVATWA
EARTH/PRITHVI	SHABDAT SPARSHAT ROOP + RASA+ GANDHA	KHARATW

Now let us understand these five elements one by one:

AKASH MAHABHUT-

It's also termed ether or space. We should not get confused by the name Akash as if it represents sky. But instead it represents space. Akash represents hollow cavities within the body and empty areas of cosmos,it helps in transmitting sound waves.Its frictionless and resistance less smooth abundant mahabhuta.It is also the body channels, pores or empty spaces. We know that every matter occupies space and every matter is made of atoms which may be loosely or compactly bound with each other, but they always have space in between. All these examples of space from modern point of view are the Akash Mahabhut of Ayurveda.

VAYU/AIR MAHABHUT:

It's gaseous form of element. It is represented as Vata Dosha, in body which is responsible for movements like that of motor or sensory nerve impulses. Conceptually anything that moves or is transported does so because of this Mahabhuta. Its light ,subtle, mobile, transparent, rough.

FIRE/AGNI MAHABHUTA:

Agni mahabhut is hot, sharp, intense, dry, light and is the major constituent of biological humour- Pitta Dosha. It is responsible for proteins that we take are bio transformed by this Agni to the substances that can be utilized by our body. Ayurveda science pays a special attention to this Agni. There is a full-fledged subject related to this Agni as KAYA CHIKITSA - where kaya means Agni So much so that Ayurvedic therapeutics focuses on rectification and maintenance of this biological Agni, Ayurveda has described the element of Agni (fire) a Mahabhuta long before the proposition of energy and matter.

WATER/JAL MAHABHUTA:

It is moist,cohesive, sticky ,cool, oily in its properties. It symbolises the liquid State. This mahabhuta is the main constituent of biological humour -Kapha Dosha. This mahabhuta is responsible for Lubrication, temperature regulation, body defence mechanism, Carrier of nutrients and other materials from one site to another etc.

EARTH /PRITHVI MAHABHUTA:

It's the solid state element .Its heavy , hard , dull , slow and dense in its properties. Its presence provides shape and weight to matter. It Symbolises shape (form), permanence, stability and rigidity. The basic property of kharatwa that it has is indicated in our body parts as teeth, bones, tissue, joints etc

Lets understand the aspect of Panchmahabhuta in disease and its cure which will help us to understand its importance Following information will be a Supporting tool in this regard:-

Panchmahabhuta means anything to everything be it living or non-living if you Know - you know its basic composition material i.e. Panchmahabhuta. Now you have to focus on the composition, quantity of these elements which is different for different things, which is the basic difference in all we see around. From here, the knowledge of Panchmahabhuta to the need for practical implementation arises.

Since our concern is not universe, it's we ourselves whom we wish to understand, through this Panchbhuta theory - let's try to put our Knowledge and information of each bhuta that we have collected to be used to have an applied approach.

The immediate perceptible form of Prithvi is Earth. In general it has been evaluated that earth has five layers. Predominance of activities of Akash and Vayu are seen in Atmosphere, Jala in hydrosphere, Agni in Mantle and core, Prithvi in lithosphere. Vayu keeps moving in all the layers.

Human body is regarded as parthivsharir and the above description is the best reason why humans are so called. There are in total 112 elements discovered out of which 26 are in human body itself.

We know that the smallest structural and functional unit of life is an atom. since according to ayurveda everything is made of panchmahabhuta -the minutest element as its basic component, lets have a brief look at the corelation among the two in an atom .The mass of electrons and protons is due to the prithvi tatv, cohesion between the particles of atom is attributed to jala mahabhuta ,the electric charge on electrons and protons is due to agni mahabhuta presence ,the force with which electrons and other particles move around the nucleus of the atom is representing vayu mahabhuta, the empty space within and around the atom is akash mahabhuta.

Modern science supports the proposition that five-tanmatras are the progenitors of their visible counterparts by describing basic Formative particles electron, proton, neutron which could be tanmatras combining in different proportions and forming atoms, elements, compounds. However Ayurvedic Tridosh theory brings Mahabhuta theory into a practical, usable, understandable format for its clinical application.

3. TRIDOSHA

TRIDOSHA

TRIDOSHA THEORY

Tridosha are the three humours or forces of the body which bring health when in equilibrium and become the underlying cause of each and every disease when imbalanced. Therefore, these three doshas are three pillars of our body. To understand their practical importance let us first have a brief look at them.

Vata Dosha-

Although all the three doshas are the basic pillars of human body still the most strong pillar or the central pillar or we can say which supports the other two pillars of Pitta Dosha and Kapha Dosha is this Vata Dosha only.

For it acharya's say-

"Pitta Pangu, Kapha Pangu, Pangvoh Maldhaatveh"

"VayunaYatr Niyantey Tatr Gachanti Meghvrat."

The balanced Vata Dosha is responsible for initiation and controlling of all the functions of body as a main leading dosha. It supervises the mind along with the body. Predominantly this dosha has air and space as its main constituents because of which it is weightless, light and free to move from here and there throughout the body controlling and managing rest others.

In the Atharva Veda it was mentioned that the derangement of three physiological factors.These factors were termed 'Sushka' 'Sikta'and "Sanchari, and these terms literally 'mean 'dry' wet, permeating respectively. In course of time they transformed into the terms 'Vayu,""Pitta and Kapha mentioned in the Tridosha.

Pitta Dosha:

This Dosha is the heat factor of our body. All the metabolic processes of digestion, absorption are through it. Mainly constituted of Agni and water this dosha is the sign of life as it maintains heat of the body and energy. Pitta is the combination of energy of fire and water, digestion, and transformation are its chief functions. When in healthy balance state, this dosha brings intelligence, charisma, courage, clarity, and the light of understanding. In excess, it can cause imbalances related to excess heat, such as anger, jealousy, irritated skin, sharp hunger, and difficulty sleeping.This dosha is symbolic of agni mahabhuta of cosmos.Its fluid nature renders it mobile.The seven qualities of *pitta* are described as slightly oily, penetrating, hot, light, odorous, free-flowing, and liquid. It also governs maintenance of body temperature, visual perception, colour and complexion of the skin, intellect and emotions

Kapha Dosh:

This dosha is the strength pillar of the body as it is responsible for the immunity. A combination of Earth and Water are the main constituents; it acts as the buffer System of our body. It helps in pacifying the excess heat of Pitta dosha and dryness of Vatadosha. It is heavy, slow, cool, sleek, smooth, delicate, thick, stable, gross, and cloudy. Kapha provides structure and robustness to all the things; it gives the cohesiveness needed to maintain a particular form. Kapha additionally hydrates all cells and frameworks, lubricates the joints, saturates the skin, maintains immunity and safeguards the tissues. Kapha is often associated with water energy, and with love and compassion.It is the basic element that holds the cells together that comprises the muscle, fat, lubricates the joints and bones in the body as well as triggers the immune response by safeguarding the tissues. An individual governed by kapha dosha is well built with strong stamina and a healthy gut. Any imbalance in this can alter functions and can cause fluid retention, allergies and fatigue.

Now from modern point of view the smallest Structural and functional unit of each body is a cell. This cell is controlled by its nucleus, which represents vata in its properties. The mitochondria and the other enzymes mediated chemical reactions taking place at cell level represents the Pitta dosha while the cell membrane and the fluid within the cell that protects the cell is all about the Kaphadosha, so to precisely understand and co relate the Ayurvedic Tridosha theory, One can easily understand it through as small a unit as cell with properties and functions similar to the ones mentioned for Tridosha.

We know that the Ayurvedic concept of Health and the modern concept of Health truly match on one thing that the State of health is State of body being in homeostasis/ equilibrium.

"समदोषःसमाग्निश्चसमधातुमलक्रियः प्रसन्नात्मेन्द्रियमनःस्वस्थतिअभिधीयते"

Now From modern point of view this homeostasis or equilibrium is maintained mainly by three Systems - (1) Nervous System (2) Endocrine System (3) Immune system working in coordination with each other.

However these three systems of modern sciences are at par to the humours of Ayurveda. i.e. Vata Dosha governs and is in accordance to the functions of nervous system.The endocrine system is at par to the functions of Pitta Dosha and Immunity is what Kapha Dosha works on in its normal State. These three systems are regarded as the three co-ordinating systems of body, just as the three humours - When functioning in equilibrium in co-ordination with each other contribute to a healthy state of mind and body.

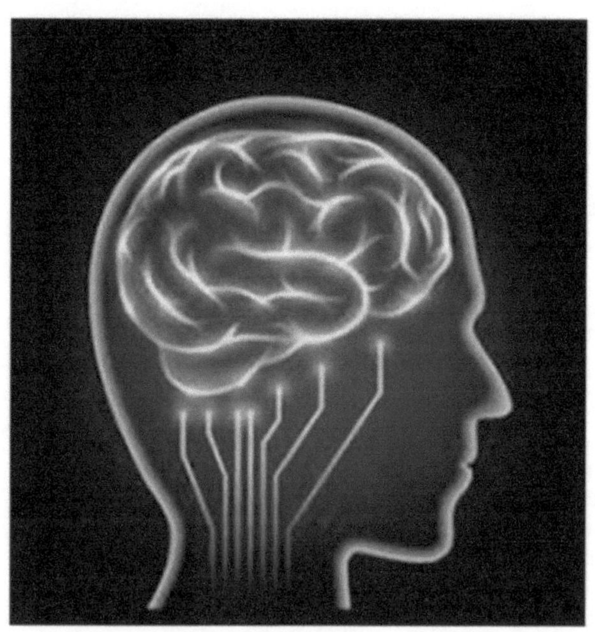

Vata Dosha is explained as

- *वायुस्तन्त्रयन्त्रधरः*
- *प्रवर्तकश्चेष्टानामुच्चावचानाम*
- *नियन्ताप्रणेताचमनसः*
- *सर्वन्द्रियाणामुयोजकः*
- *सर्वेन्द्रियार्थानामभिवोढ़ा*
- *संधानकरःशरीरस्य*
- *समीरोडग्रे*
- *प्रवर्तकोनाच :*
- *हर्षोत्साहयोर्योनिः*
- *दोषसंशोषणः*
- *क्षेप्ताबहिर्मलानाम्*
- *कर्तागर्भाकृतिनाम्*

- स्थूलाणुस्रोतसांभेत्ता

All these above shlokas indicate the importance and inevitable impact of vayu in controlling all the bodily activities just the way Nervous system Co-ordinates and controls all the functions of the body.

The word "Vayu" is formed from "Vaa Gati Gandhanyo"

Gati- means movement, knowledge

Gandhana - means reflection of enthusiasm, respond to stimulus

Combining meanings of gati and gandhana, it is clear that the entire spectrum of sensory and motor functions, physical and motor abilities of an individual, reflexes to stimulus and all activities happening in body are under control of balanced Vata i.e. vata is a remote controller of all functions just like nervous system controlling, commanding and co-ordinating all the bodily activities.For this reason vayu is regarded as prana. Now let's understand the functions of vata as nervous controller in respect to its five sub types.

PRANA VATA

प्राणेऽत्र मूर्धगः ।

उरः कंठचरो बुद्धिहृदयेन्द्रियचित्तधृक्
॥

ष्ठीवनं क्षवथूदगारनिःश्वासान्नप्रवेशकृत् । ।

अ० हृ० सू० 12/4/

According to the above Shloka, this pranvata is situated in the head and co-ordinates and controls functions of reflexes such as Sneezing, belching, deglutition and is controlling the intellect, cardiovascular and sense organs functions.

Among five vata dosha, prana vayu is situated in the head and travel across urah (thorax region) and kantha (throat region). It is reasonable for functioning of spitting, sneezing, eructation, respiration, and deglutition and also maintains the proper functioning of budhhi (intelligence/judgement), hridaya (heart), chitta (mind). Here head refers to brain and brain stem as it controls all these functions. All the functions of pranavayu are compared as per modern medical science. Basically, the functions of limbic system,cranial nerves, cerebral cortex, basal ganglia and other structures might be compared with the functions of prana vata. So we can easily understand the basic principles of Ayurveda which is badly required in this present era. Most of the vatik disorders discussed in Ayurveda are being diagnosed under neurological disorders in modern medicine. Very few works have been achieved on conceptual features of vata. In this article an attempt has been made to correlate the physiological activity of prana vayu with special reference to neurophysiology. For this study, the basic materials have been collected from the Āyurvedic classics with the available commentaries, as well as text books of contemporary science have been referred for better understanding of the concept and its comparison with contemporary science The primary site of Prana Vayu is head.Here is an attempt to compare the function of Prana Vayu with its modern aspect as per contemporary science.

नाभिस्थः प्राणपवनः स्पृष्ट्वा हृत्कमलान्तरम् । कण्ठाद्बहिर्विनिर्याति पातुं विष्णपदामृतम् ।। • पीत्वा चाम्बरपीयूषं पुनरायाति वेगतः । प्रीणयन्देहमखिलं जीवं च जठरानलम् ।।शा० पू० 5/44, 45

STHIVANA:

Sthivana means the function of spitting. It is the action of ejection of saliva or other substance from the mouth which is conducted by nucleus of facial nerve. It is the seventh cranial nerve containing sensory, motor and parasympathetic nerve.The sensory fiber carries the sensation of taste from the anterior 2/3rd of the tongue to brain. The somatic motor fibers of seventh cranial nerve supply the muscle of facial expression and muscle of scalp. Its nucleus is located in the pons. The parasympathetic fibers arise from the superior salivary nucleus and supply to sub mandibular as well as sublingual salivary gland

KSHAVATHU:

Kshavathu means the function of sneezing.It means to throw out mucus containing foreign particles or irritants and cleanse the nasal cavity. It is reflex action when any dust particles disturbs the nasal passage. A reflex action contains of a receptor, a sensory nerve, an integrating center, a motor nerve, and an effector. The receptors which are nerve ending in the nasal pathways detect an irritant. Maxillary branch of trigeminal nerve transport these impulses to sneezing center of brain stem.The sneezing center sends the information to facial nerve along with the nerves that lead to lungs and diaphragm. Then eyes begin watering, nasal mucosa secretes fluid, diaphragm moves to take a deep breath. Then the muscle in the chest contracts and it causes the air to leave the nose and mouth suddenly. The whole function is under control of both trigeminal and facial nerve11.

UDGARA:

Udgara means belching reflex which is a polysynaptic visceral reflex. It is found in a period of less than two second. It is formed of three independent reflex responses. Due to contraction of lower esophagus and diaphragm there is inhibition of the muscle barrier between the stomach and esophagus. It is the first belching reflex. This reflex is triggered by air causing tension in the muscle fibers of the wall of stomach that is under the esophagus. So the air bolus rapidly escapes into the lower esophagus which is under pressure from the stomach wall. This reflex is determined by the brain through the vagus nerve. The rapid movement of air into the lower esophagus concurrently activates the other two reflexes. The inhibition of the muscle barrier between the esophagus and pharynx is the second belch reflex. It is developed by pharyngeal muscles. This reflex also activates muscles whose main function is to pull the esophago-pharyngeal barrier open. It is the rapid air movement across the pharynx that causes the sound of the belch. This reflex is also mediated by the brain through the vagus nerve. At the same time, the third belch reflex is activated. It begins a contraction wave of the upper esophagus which moves upward toward the mouth bringing the air bolus to the top of the esophagus. This reflex is possibly decided by the spinal cord. The result of these two reflexes is to propel the air bolus from the lower esophagus into the oral cavity. The area postrema which is in the medulla or hind brain primarily controls the belch response

SWASA:

Swasa means the process of respiration.Group of neurons which is located bilaterally in the medulla oblongata and pons of brain stem are the respiratory center in brain. It is branched into three major colons of neurons. A dorsal respiratory group which is situated in the dorsal portion of medulla and it causes inspiration. A ventral respiratory group which is located in ventero lateral part of medulla mainly causes expiration. The pneumotaxic center which is present dorsally in the superior portion of pons mainly controls rate and depth of breathing.

ANNA PRAVESHA:

It consists of mastication, salivation and deglutination. The fifth cranial nerve i.e. trigeminal nerve is a mixed type of nerve.The motor fibers which supply the muscle of mastication arise from the nucleus in the pons. The seventh cranial nerve i.e. facial nerve contains sensory, motor and parasympathetic fibers. The parasympathetic fibers arise from the superior salivary nucleus and supply the submandibular and sublingual salivaryglands. The 9th cranial nerve i.e. glosspharyngeal nerve contain sensory, motor and parasympathetic fibers. The motor fibers arise from the nucleus ambigus situated in medulla and supply the stylopharyngeal muscle. The 10th cranialnerve i.e. vagus nerve contain sensory, motor and parasympathetic fibers. The somatic efferent fibers arise from the nucleus ambigus and supply the laryngeal and pharyngeal muscle. The 11th nerve (accessory) is purely motor nerve. Its spinal root supplies the sternocleidomastoid and trapezius muscle whereas its bulbar root supplies some of the muscle of larynx, pharynx, and soft palate. The 12th cranial nerve i.e.hypoglossal nerve contains ony motor fibers arises from the medulla. It supplies the muscle of tongue.The sensitive tactile areas of the posterior mouth and pharynx are present in a ring around the pharyngeal opening. It helps to initiate the pharyngeal stage of swallowing. Impulses are transmitted from these areas into the medulla oblongata, either into or closely associated with the tractus solitarious through the sensory portions of trigeminal and glossopharyngeal nerves. Then the medulla oblongata receives all sensory impulses from the mouth. The stages of the swallowing process are started by the medulla and lower portion of the pons. The areas in the medulla and lower pons are called as the swallowing center. The motor impulses are transmitted by 5th, 9th,10th and12th cranial nerve15.

HRIDAYA DHARANA:

It holds the function of heart. The parasympathetic motor fibers of vagusnerve, arise from the dorsal motor nucleus situated in the floor of fourth ventricle, in medulla. The fibers supply the viscera of thorax (heart and lungs) and the gut in upper abdomen. Vasomotor center controls the activity of heart. Whenever there is a need to increase heart rate and contractility, the lateral portion of vasomotor center transmits excitatory impulses through the sympathetic nerve fibers to the heart. On the contrary the vasomotor center sends signal to the adjacent dorsal motor nuclei of vagus nerve whenever there is a require to decrease heart pumping, which then transmit parasympathetic impulses through the vagus nerves to the heart. It causes decrease of heart rate and heart contractility. Therefore the vasomotor center has an important role in either increase or decrease heart activity. Every part of the reticular substance of pons, mesencephalon and diencephalon carries large number of small neurons. These neurons can either excite or inhibit the vasomotor center. The vasoconstrictorsystem is controlled by hypothalamus. It brings powerful excitatory or inhibitory effects on the vasomotor center. The vasomotor center can also be excited or inhibited by many parts of the cerebralcortex. The vasomotor center is excited by stimulation of the motor cortex because the impulses are transmitted downward into hypothalamus and then to the vasomotor center. Also stimulation of anterior temporal lobe, the orbital areas of the frontal cortex, the anterior part of the cingulated gyrus, the amygdale, the septum and the hippocampus can either excite or inhibit the vasomotor center. These are depending upon the precise

UDANA VATA

"उरःस्थानमुदानस्यनासानाभिगलांश्चरेत्वाक्प्रवृतिःप्रयत्नोज

बलवर्णस्मृतिक्रियः॥"अं.ह. सू. 12/5.

This Vata is situated in the chest region. The functions of this Vata includes speech production, It helps in memorising Vocabulary for well-articulated speech, initiation to Speak, volume to voice are the functions of this vata. that means the speech centre of brain is also. Co-ordinated and controlled by Udana Vayuas this centre is responsible for meaningful speech. Udana vayu performs its function with the help coordination and cooperation of prana and vyana vayu.

Vakpravritti and Varnasmriti:

The most important function of Udana vayu is production of speech. It also helps in singing which is alsoa type of vakpravritti. Varnasmriti refers to the process of recall of vocabulary. Recalling the vocabulary is required to frame a meaningful sentences during Vakpravritti. Varna means vocabulary. Smriti is also the function of Udanavayu as it helps in regulating the function of speech. Areas in the brain that play important role in processing of language and speech. These areas are called receptive area and executive area. Receptive area is also called sensory speech area. They are wernicke's area that perform the perception of spoken language and the angular gyrus that subserve the perception of written language. Area 41 and 42 are also included in receptive areas the executive area initiates the production speech. These are Broca's area (area 44,area 45) and writing area. Broca's area is concerned with motor aspect of speech Broca's area regulates the function of muscles of lip, tongue, pharynx and larynx. Exner writing area is located in the posterior part of the frontal lobe. This area helps in writing after visual perception of word.

VYANA

VAYU

व्यानोहर्दिस्थितःकृत्सनदेहचारीमहाजवःगत्यपक्षेपणोत्क्षेपनिमेषोन्मेषणादिकाः प्रायः सर्वाः क्रियास्तस्मिन्प्रतिबद्धाःशरीरिणाम्"

vyana vayu is responsible for various movements taking place in our body. It performs the

function of rasa rakta sambahana . it is responsible for all the bodily movements.All movements are effected through

contraction and relaxation of muscle. It performs its function by proper coordination and cooperation other vayu

All types of Vata while execuiting their functions are interdependent on each other.e.g. Prana vata performs the function of ingestion of food. Vyana vata helps in the perception of taste (anna aswadan) If the pleasant flavor of food is not worked with the help of vyana vayu (annaswadana) it will be vomited. Hence function of prana need cooperation of vyana

vayu.similarly Srotovisodhana and samvahan is the function of vyan vayu through this, it reaches to tissue level.but

nutrient portion at tissue level is because of Srotoprinana which is the function of udana vayu .so,this function is performed by the vyana vayu with the help of udana vayu.

Functions of vayan vayu in Modern aspect

Gati:

Gati means movement. Cerebrum, brain stem and spinal cord all these three are responsible for all

type of simple and complex type of movement.

(1) the primary motor cortex,generates mostly discrete pattern of movement.
(2) the premotor area cause much more complex patters of movements and (3) the supplementary motor area

Stimulates bilateral movement rather than

unilateral for example bilateral grasping movement

Cerebellum helps sequence the motor activities and makes the corrective adjustments in the body's motor activities while they are being executed so that they will conform to the motor signals directed by cerebral motor cortex and other parts of the brain.

Nimesha:

It includes the closing and opening of eyelids. The eyelid muscle is supplied by three cranial nerve

(3rd, 5th, 7th) and sympathetic nerve fibers. The occulomotor nerve has somatic efferent fibers

arising in the occulomotor nucleus supply all extrinsic muscle of eyeball Opthalamic branch of

trigeminal nerve supply to muscle of eye which is responsible for closing of eyelid. Sympathetic

fibers contribute to upper eyelid retraction by innervations of superior tarsal muscle contributing to

lower lid retraction.

Rasasambahana and Asrik sravana:

Rasasambahana is one of the most important functions of vyana vayu which means continous circulation of rasa in cyclic order. The function Asrik Sravana is possible by the stimulation of the sympathetic supply to heart.

Vyana makes Rasa to get forcefully ejected out of the heart and makes it circulate throughout the

body. So, sympathetic and parasympathetic control of heart can be included under Vyana Vata.

Sympathetic function in the medulla oblongata, which is concerned with the control of heart, is

vasomotor centre. Hypothalamus and other cortical areas in turn influence this. Similarly nucleus

ambigus is the parasympathetic center. Vyana Vata is indicative of all these functional entities.

Sweda sravana:

Sweat gland is a tubular structure. It consists of two parts. First a deep subdermal coiled portion that

secrete sweat and second a duct portion that passes outward through the dermis and epidermis of the

skin. The secretory portion of the sweat gland secretes a fluid called the primary secretion or

precursor secretion. Stimulation of anterior hypothalamus preoptic area in the brain causes sweating

'प्रायःसर्वाःक्रियास्तस्मिन्प्रतिबद्धाःशरीरिणाम् '

Samana Vayu:

समानोअग्निःसमीपस्थःकोष्ठेचरतिसर्वतःअन्नंगृह्णातिपचतिविवेचयतिमुंचति”अ. ह. सा/ 8

The site of this vayu as per its properties mentioned in the Shloka is the Gastro intestinal tract. Its functions co-relate to the functions of enteric nervous system. This vayu plays role in receiving food from the mouth, digestion, absorption, segregation and finally expulsion out of waste food material. All this involves movements of hypoglossal muscle swallowing centre of medulla, Peristaltic movement of GIT. The function of Samanvayu can be compared to stretch reflex and parasympathetic system.

Saman vayu is present near jatharagni (digestive fire) and stimulates the Agni(pachak agni) for pachan of food and its conversion into saar kitta bhaag . with the help of Apana vayu waste producs are eliminated from body. All the functions of samanavayu can be compared with physiological functions of anatomical structure of contemporary modern medical science.

Functions of vayan vayu in respect of its modern aspect:

ANNAM GRIHNATI:

Annam means food ,grihnati means recieves/holds this function of . Samana vayu is done by the coordinative

function of Prana vayu.Annam grihnati means Deglutition in modern science,which is a complicated mechanism. It

involves 3 stages.

1. Voluntary stage of swallowing:

The pressure of upward and backward movements of tongue against the

palate causes squeezing of food into pharynx posteriorly. Twelfth cranial nerve (hypoglossal nerve) is supplied to the

muscle of tongue.

2. Involuntary pharyngeal stage of swallowing:

After squeezing of bolus to posterior mouth and pharynx, the epithelial swallowing receptor areas around the pharynx are stimulated. Then the impulses are transmitted through the sensory portions of trigeminal and glossopharyngeal nerve

into medulla oblongata. The motor impulse from swallowing center to pharynx and esophagus are transmitted by 5th,9th, 10th, 12th cranial nerve.

3. Esophageal stage of swallowing:

The esophagus exhibits two types of peristaltic movement i.e. propulsive and mixing movements. These peristaltic waves are initiated and controlled by intrinsic neuronal circuits in the myentric nervous system.

ANNAM PACHATI:

Annam pachati means digests the food but we pretty well know that digestion and metabolism of food is thechief function of agni. so, samana vayu is to stimulate the agni for digestion and metabolism. So all factors which stimulate the agni for digestion and metabolism comes under the annam pachati function of saman vayu.

ANNAM VIVECHAYATI:

vivaychti means separation of saara from kitta and absorption of saar bhaag.in modern science the saar part

is absorbed by the process of osmosis, active transport of sodium from epithelial cells. glucose by sodium glucose cotransporter, protein by sodium amino acid co- transporter, absorption of calcium by

parathyroid hormone.

MUNCHATI:

It means elimination of kitta i.e. fecal matters and urine. Elimination the function of Apana

vayuso Samanavayu initiates Apana vayu to execute its function for the expulsion of waste product. This is due to coordinated functions of both Apana vayu and Samana vayu. it initiates both defecation and micturition reflex.When a mass movement forces feces into rectum, desire for defecation occurs immediately. Two type of reflex is seen. One is an intrinsic reflex mediated by local ENS in the rectal wall causes peristalsis from descending colon to sigmoid and rectum.These waves cause the relaxation of internal sphincter. At the same time if the external anal sphincter is open defecation occurs. The other defecation reflex is initiated by parasympathetic nervous system. After entering of fecal matter into the rectum, the nerve endings in the rectum are stimulated then signal transmitted to the spinal cord. Reflex signal via pelvic nerve goes to descending colon, sigmoid and rectum. These parasympathetic signals travel in the pelvic nerve and greatly intensify peristalsis and relax the internal anal sphincter. Micturition reflex is due to stretch reflex. When bladder begins to fill urine at higher pressure, sensory stretch receptors in the bladder wall are initiated to send signals to the sacral segment of cord through pelvic nerve. Then it reflexively back again to bladder through the parasympathetic nerve fibers and causes micturition.this function too is done by coordination of saman vayu and apan vayu.

Apana Vayu:

"अपानोऽअपानग:श्रोणिबस्तिमेदोरुगोचरशुक्रार्तवशकृन्मूत्रगर्भनिष्क्रमणक्रिय "अ. ह. स 12/ 9

ApanaVayu functions are similar to the functions described for Autonomic Nervous System. Situated in the pelvic region the processes of ejaculation, micturition, menstruation, defecation, parturition all come under the control of this Vayu.Apana vayu is located in pakvadhana and traversed though sroni (pelvis), basti (urinary bladder), medhra (external genital apparatus of each sex) and uru (thighs). It helps in elimination samirana (flatus), sakrit (faeces), mutra (urine), sukra (semen), garbha (fetus), artava (menstrual fluid)

Functions of apana vayu in Modern Aspects:

Sukra Niskramana:

Sukra niskraman means the ejaculation of semen caused by parasympathetic impulses that pass from sacral region of spinal cord through pelvic nerve to penis. When the sexual stimulus becomes extremely intense means parasympathetic impulses are at peak level, the reflex center of the spinal cord emit sympathetic impulses that leave the cord at T12 to L2 and pass to the genital organs through the hypogastric and pelvic sympathetic nerve plexuses to initiate emission.

Mutra Niskramana:

It means micturition. It is is initiated by stretch reflex. When urine begins to fill in the bladder higher pressure, sensory stretch receptors in the bladder wall are stimulated and send

signals to the sacral segment of cord through pelvic nerve. Then it reflexively back again to bladder

through motor parasympathetic nerve fibers to causes micturition. It involves coordination between

central, autonomic and somatic nervous system.and according to ayurveda saman vayu vayan vayu and apan vayu in coordination meet out mutra nishkraman.

Mala Niskramana:

It is act of defecation. stimulated by mass movement of feces into the rectum. Two type of reflex iactions are responsible for it. One is an intrinsic reflex which is mediated by local

ENS in the rectal wall. The other defecation reflex is initiated by parasympathetic nervous system. After entering of fecal matter into the rectum, the nerve endings in

the rectum are stimulated then signal transmitted to the spinal cord through afferent nerve fiber.

Reflex signal via pelvic nerve goes to descending colon, sigmoid and rectum.

Artava Niskramana:

It is menstruation. The vasoconstriction due to prostaglanddin leads to hypoxia which results in necrosis of endometrium. Due to necrosis, the blood vessels of endometrium start rupturing and blood oozes out.

Garbha Nishkramana:

The Garbha nishkramana delivery of baby. In the end of pregnancy the uterus develops strong rhythmic contraction that the baby is expelled. . Increased estrogen to progesterone ratio towards the end of the pregnancy is partly responsible for

the increased contractility of the uterus. Stimulation of paraventricular nuclei of hypothalamus causes neurohypophysis to secrete oxytocin hormone which causes uterine contraction.

Now let's further understand this co-relation in a simpler manner. Your nervous system is what? Basically it's the commanding officer who gives commands through brain and instructs your body to control its various movements, thoughts, automatic responses to the world around you in form of reflexes, controls the organ systems - plans the appropriate time for secretion of various hormones , your sleeping and awaking, your appetite your thirst - all you do, you think, you say, you feel, Your memory retains – everything is under one command and i.e. your Nervous System- if you look at the vast functions and properties mentioned about the powerful DoshaVata - the whole functions narrated of Nervous system would be self-explanatory to understand their correlation and drag a conclusion that What nervous System does in modern science Vata dosha does in Ayurvedic concept. Just as although Controller of every action Nervous System doesn't functions alone same is the story of Vata-though being the most powerful of the three yet it works in co-ordination with its other two humours – Moreover just as the neurons of nervous system are present all throughout the body same is with Vata Dosha, it is also present all through the body giving commands controlling and coordinating with dosha, dhaatu ,mala, Aatma and Mana.

PITTA

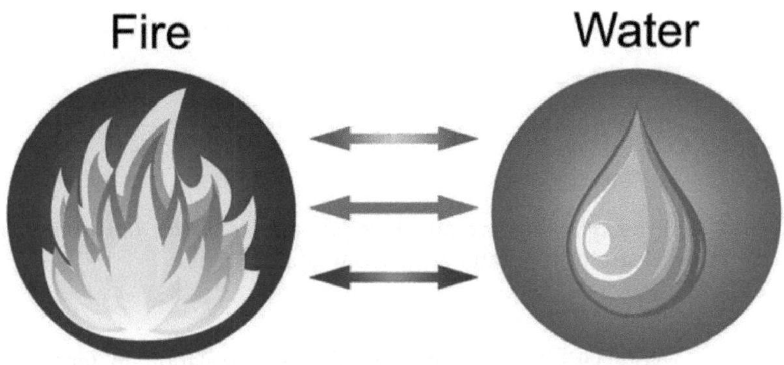

Pitta word originated from the word tap santapey that means the one which heats , the one which is the cause of generation of energy, transformation of things [as heat is the essential requirement for any transformation] although everything in the universe is panchbhautik yet the energy driven in universe is due to the Tejasmahabhut of the panchmahabhut responsible for bio transformative activities these similar properties of Tejasmahaboot are comprised in body by the pitta dosha. Hormones cause bio transformative activities similar to Tejasmahabhuta and pitta dosha, this similarity and core relation between the endocrine system and the pitta dosha is also because of the similar properties they share with each other.Hormones like the pitta dosha are Ushna, tikshna, suksham, laghu, vishad , daha, paka, prabha, prakash and varnaka.

Now let us understand the properties of hormones in respect to pitta dosa

Ushna[hot]

There are hormones which increase body heat for example progesterone, thyroxin ,HCG

Tikshna [penetrating power]

Steroid hormones have this property as they can penetrate through cell membrane.

Suksham (Microscopic).

A very small concentration of hormones reaches its target cells and affect the intracellular metabolism to modify the Cell Junction eg.Glucagon, Growth hormone, Testosterone, Oestrogen, Vasopressin.

Laghu (low molecular weight):

Some hormones work quickly e.g. epinephrine (adrenaline)

Ruksha (Cunctous):

Thromboxane A2 causes vasoconstriction

Vishad (Detergent):

Prostaglandins are anti Lipolytic agents These hormones inhibit the release of free fatty acids from adipose tissue.

Now let's further understand this co-relation in terms of the subtle types of Pitta :-.

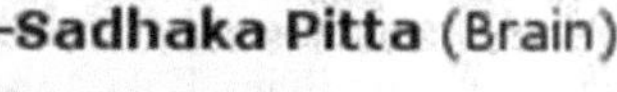

PACHAK PITTA

तच्चादृष्टहेतुकेन विशेषेण पक्वामाशयमध्यस्थं पित्तं चतुर्विधमन्नपानं पचति, विवेचयति च दोषरसमूत्रपुरीषाणि तत्रस्थमेव चात्मशक्त्या शेषाणां पित्तस्थानानां शरीरस्य चाग्निकर्मणाऽनुग्रहं करोति, तस्मिन् पित्तेपाचकोऽग्निरिति संज्ञा ।सु वू० 21/9

From the above shloka of acharya Sushrut it is clear that Pachak pitta is situated in the GI tract between Stomach and intestine. The above mentioned functions of this pitta co-relates to the G.I. tract enzymes amlyolitic ,proteolytic, lipolyticetc and hormones CCK, gastrin, secretin, histamine, somatostatin etc.

Functions of pachak pitta in respect to modern science

AHARA PACHANA AND AHARA RASA FORMATION

Aahara pachan is the property of pachak pitta which is also called jatharagni or pachakagni .

Seat of Pachaka Pitta is the site between Pakwashaya and Amashaya i.e Grahani or Pittadhara Kala.Aahar pachan also called as Digestion is responsible for breakdown of complex food into simpler form. It begins from the mouth till small intestine the process of digestion continues. from functional point of view grahni is the duodenum of modern science.

NOURISHES VARIOUS PITTA STHANA

Pachaka pitta does pachan of food and divideds it into saar and kitta bhaag,

the saar bhaag is full of nutrients amd other important minerals which circulate as saara through out the body providing nourishment to all the pitta. Pachaka pitta is compared with digestive enzymes that help in digestion of food material.

- Ranjaka pitta which resides in yakrit and pliha help in

coloration of rasa dhatu means the formation of rakta dhatu. Factors regulating erythropoiesis and maturation of RBCs are

vitamin B12, folic acid, pyridoxine, Vitamin C (helps iron absorption), minerals like iron, copper which mainly comes

from diet. If the digestion of food is not occurred properly vitamin B12, iron, folic acid and others cannot absorb

properly.

- Sadhaka pitta which resides in hridaya helps in fulfilling the desires of mind. If there is improper digestion, ajirna will

occur. During ajirna bhrama, murchha like symptoms are appeared so that function of sadhak pitta is hampered.

- Alochaka pitta which resides in dristhi (eye) helps in perception of vision. Vitamin A is present in both cytoplasm of the rods and in the pigment layer of retina. Vitamin A is responsible for formation of Rhodospin.

- Bhrajaka pitta which resides in twak helps in digestion and absorption of substance that is being used in mardan,

sechana, avagahana and expression of shades in the skin. Mainly pachaka pitta is responsible for all chemical reaction.

It helps bhrajaka pitta for this type of function. Dhatavagni depend upon pachakagni. Aggravation and diminution of

pachakagni results in the aggravation and diminution of other agni. Pachaka pitta helps in the formation of nutrient

products which is used for the nourishment of every cell. After the proper growth of the cell bhrajak pitta perform its

function. The substance which is lipid in nature enters the cell nmembrane of the cell.

ABSORPTION OF AAHAR RASA

After the intake of aahara, it moves towards the kostha by the help of prana vayu. The site of pachakagni is grahani or

pakvamashaya better known as pittadhara kala. Samana vayu which is present in amashaya stimulate the pachakagni for the digestion and separation of food as well as shoshyati i.e., absorption of water and nutrients15. This absorption of nutrient and water requires movement which is the main function of vata.

So here both samana vata and pachakagi is responsible for

absorption.

RANJAKA PITTA:

यत्तु यकृत्प्लीनोः पित्तं तस्मिन् रञ्जकोऽग्निरिति संज्ञासरसस्य रागकृदुक्तः ।। (सु.सू.21/9)

The site of Ranjaka Pitta is spleen and liver according to acharya sushrut. Here the action of ranjak pitta on aahar ras transforms it into Rakta dhatu. Erythropoeisis occurs in liver at foetal life, where as storage of RBC and their formation in spleen in adult life takes place according to modern science there by the two sites of sushrut ranjak pitta are in accordance with modern view. Vagbhattas site of Ranjaka Pitta is आमाशय which is equally a justified site, as its the sight of Gastric intrinsic factor which is required for absorption of vitamin B12, which in turn is needed for DNA synthesis of RBC precursors

Modern aspects of ranjak pitta functions

Erythropoiesis is the process of formation of red blood cells. In the early week of embryonic life red blood cells are produced in yolk sac. Spleen can release 100 ml of blood into other area of circulation by decreasing its size sufficiently. The sinuses of liver can release about 450 milliliters of blood into remainder of circulation. Spleen has two areas for storing blood -venous sinuses and pulp. The red pulp of the spleen is a special reservoir that contains large quantities

of concentrated red blood cells. These red blood cells can be expelled into general circulation whenever sympathetic nervous system becomes excited and causes the spleen and its vessels to contract. 50 ml of concentrated red blood cell can be released into circulation.

The cells of circulation blood are derived from pluripotential hematopoietic stem cell in bone marrow.Growth and reproduction of different stems cells are controlled by multiple proteins called growth inducers.Differentiation inducers are the proteins that promote differentiation of cells. As the function of raktagni is to synthesize the rakta dhatu so the function of Growth inducers and Differentiation inducers comes under the function of Raktagni.Erythropoietin enhances red blood cell production. Thus the function of Erythropoietin comes under the function of Raktagni.

Norepinephrine, epinephrine and several of prostaglandin stimulate kidney for erythropoietin production.The effect of testosterone to increase red blood cell production may be at least partly indirect because of the

increased metabolic rate that occurs after testosterone administration. So norpeinephrine, epinephrine, prostaglandin, testosterone have an important role in erythrocyte production. So the function of norepinephrine, epinephrine, prtostaglandin, and androgens are come under the functions of raktagni.

The parietal cells of the gastric gland secrete a glycoprotein called intrinsic factor, which combine with vitamin B12 in food and makes it available for absorption by the gut. Intrinsic factor binds tightly with vitamin B12. In this bound state vitamin B12 is protected from digestion by gastrointestinal secretion. Intrinsic factor binds to specific receptor site on the brush border membrane of the mucosal cells of ileum. A common cause of red blood

cell maturation failure is failure to absorb vitamin B12 from gastrointestinal tract. In diseases like atrophic gastric mucosa stomach fails to produce normal gastric secretions. Lack of intrinsic factor decreases the availability of vitamin B12 and failure in maturation of RBCs. So, the functions of intrinsic factor come under the function of ranjak pitta.

BHRAJAK PITTA

यत् त्वचि पित्तं तस्मिन् भ्राजकोऽग्निरिति संज्ञा । सोऽभ्यङ्गपरिषेकावगाहावलेपनादीनां क्रियाद्रव्याणां पक्ता, छायानां च प्रकाशकः ।।: *(सु. सू. 21/9)*

The term Bhrajaka is derived from "Bhrajja" Dhatu which means Kaanti or the one which
maintains the natural complexion of skin. The seat of Bhrajak pitta is skin. The topical applications of oils or other herbs etc on the skin are absorbed by enzymes under skin just as the properties of bhrajak pitta. The pigmentation of skin is under the control of hormones like ACTH and MSH. So the functions of Bhrajak pitta are in line with the functions of hormones ACTH and MSH along with the skin enzymes. AcharyaCharak has accepted the view of Marichi that prakrat and vikrat complexion of skin depends on the Prakrat&Vikrat functioning of Pitta.
AcharayaSushruta has described Bhrajaka Pitta in the form of BhrajakaAgni and has accepted skin as its
Adhishtana. Bhrajaka Pitta is present in the skin, thus it absorbs the substance used in the process of Abhyanga, Avasechana, Avagahana and Aalepa.Responsible for perspiration, wetting and shining of skin and maintenance of body temperature and the natural colour of skin. In the 'Deepika' a commentary of ShrangdharaSamhita, Acharya Aadhmalla has stated that BhrajakaPitta digest the substances applied on skin and makes the skin glow due to Ushna Guna present in it. According to AcharyaSharangdhara the skin is indication only to its outermost layer i.e., Avabhasini, it
means out of seven layers of skin only the Avabhasini contributes in performing the above
functions. Other layers perform functions which are different form Avabhasini's function

Modern aspect:-
skin colour will relies on pigments such as Melanin, Haemoglobin and Carotene. The number of Melanin reasons the skin's colour to differ from faded yellow to reddish-brown to black. Melanocytes: Only Melanin producing cells in the physique The quantity of

Melanin produced and transferred to Keratinocytes determines the variations in pores and

skin colour. Melanocytes synthesize Melanin from the amino acid Tyrosine in the presence of an enzyme referred to as Tyrosinase in the organelle referred to as Melanosome .Melanocyte Stimulating Hormone (MSH): MSH is secreted via the intermediate lobe of the Pituitary gland.An expansion in MSH will reason the darkening of the pores and skin colour Cushing's syndrome due to extra ACTH may also additionally purpose hyperpigmentation(Acanthosis nigricans).

Hemoglobin that circulates in the cutaneous blood vessels play a necessary function in the colouration of the skin. Skin becomes Pale,when haemoglobin content material decreases.

SADHAK PITTA:

बुद्धिमेधाऽभिमानाद्यैरभिप्रेतार्थसाधनात् । साधकं हृदयगतं पित्तम् ।। (अ.सू.12/4)

Sadhak Pitta is situated in the heart . These functions can be recognized as functions of higher center of brain which is carried out by small molecule, rapidly acting transmitters and neuropeptides or slowly acting neurotransmitters All the functions of Sadhak pitta are psychosomatic, Psychosocial. All these functions are of cerebrum, hypothalamus, CNS and limbic.

Norepinephrinehormone is "Fight flight" hormone which acts on heart as cardiac stimulant. Along with it serotonin and Dopamine are other neurotransmitters that are included under Sadhak Pitta - because of their functions similar to that of Sadhak Pitta.

Modern aspects

The functions of sadhaka pitta as mentioned in ayurvedic texts are to achieve the intended objects with Buddhi (intelligence) Medha (discriminative ability) Abhimana (self-esteem). Sadhaka pitta also helps to achieve one's manorath and purushartha.. Acharya Chakrapani has mentioned Mana and atma is situated in hridaya and the knowledge of Sukha,

Dukha etc is achieved by atma in hridaya. In modern science it has been mentioned, emotions are developed by limbic system in brain because function of mind (mana) is regulated by brain (cortex). These emotions influence the heart. It is well known; all pleasant or unpleasant emotions influence the heart. This is due to the chemicals release in brain during emotions. Buddhi is one of the functions of sadhaka pitta. Buddhi is developed as a complex process of Chintya (thought), Vicharya (consideration), uhya (hypothesis), dheya (attention) andsankalpya (determination). In modern science a thought results from a "pattern" of stimulation of the cerebral cortex, thalamus,limbic system, and upper reticular formation of the brain stem Mana (Mind) is active but devoid of consciousness, while the Atma (soul) is conscious but not active. Ichha (Desire), Dvesha (envy), Sukha (happiness), Dukha (misery), Prayatna (effort), Chetana (consciousness), Dhriti (stability), Buddhi (intellect), Smriti (memory) and Ahankara (ego) are perceived by atma. These signs are available in all living beings which proofs the existence of atma. All these functions are higher mental functions of brain. To perceive this neurotransmitter and neuropeptides are responsible and it does at molecular level. It is responsible for communication between neurons of brain andother parts of the body. As a result, sourya, harsha, utsaha, buddhi, medha, abhimana occurs which is the function of sadhaka pitta. By the help of buddhi, medha and abhimana all the motor functions are performed to achieve the person's desire Sadhaka pitta helps in development of unbiased buddhi only when satva guna is dominant and kapha and tamo guna are in recessive state. Sadhaka pitta removes the kapha and tama and increases the satva guna and enables the Manas to perceive the things clearly.. This helps to achieve a person's own desire by following Chaturvarga.

Role of Sadhaka pitta in mental health

Acharya Charaka has mentioned in pandu roga, due to Krodha, Kama, Chinta, Bhaya, Krodhahridaystha pitta is aggravated and spread all over the body by vata dosha. Sadhaka pitta helps us to fulfill both our goals in life. Disturbed Prana vata and Sadhaka pitta may lead to psychosomatic disturbances. When homeostatic condition of Sadhaka pitta is disturbed due to aggravation of Pitta, hyperactivity impatience and anger may be seen. When it is low, the normal functions of energy transformation process, emotions thoughts and feeling may be low. Imbalance of Sadhaka pitta causes many disorders related to thought proce

AALOCHAK PITTA:

यद्दृष्ट्यां पित्तं तस्मिन्नालोचकोऽग्निरिति संज्ञा । स रूपग्रहणाधिकृतः ।।
(सु.सू.21/9)

The seat for this pitta is in eyes and it is responsible for normal vision. The neurotransmitters involved in the visual pathway can be considered as Aalochak Pitta.Alochaka Pitta is represented by the

pigments of retina viz rhodopsin, iodopsin and melanin. Rods and cones which are present in retina are responsible for colour vision and for the perception of shape and bright image. AcharyanBhela described two types of Alochaka Pitta.
1. Chakshur Vaisheshika Alochak Pitta
2. Buddhi Vaisheshika Alochak Pitta

1. CHAKSHUR VAISHESHIKA ALOCHAK PITTA

This component of Alochaka Pitta is confined to eye i.e. only anatomical eye. The visual perception takes place after coordination of these components.

· Chakshuindriyaartha - contact with the objects
· Chakshuindriya - visual perception of image of the object.
· Manas - discrimination of visual object by mind.
· Ahankara - Egoism imparts the dominance and claim to perceive the things.
· Buddhi - Intellect judgement of accepting or not.
· Atma - Soul will experience the perception after being associated with mind.

2. BUDDHI VAISHESHIKA ALOCHAKPITTA

This site of Alochaka Pitta is s beyond the eyes in brain. It perceives the minute and extraordinary matters produced in Atma(consciousness). This part of alochak Pitta enables in retention of gathered information in mind. Memorizing the past events,imagines the events that are likely to happen in future and creates imaginary events as if they have taken place now at present.Expresses the thoughts, which it has received and retained in it.

· PHYSIOLOGY OF VISION IN MODERN ASPECT

Visual process is the series of actions that take place during visual perception. During visual process, image of an object focused on retina, resulting in the production of visual perception of that object. When the image of an object in environment is focused on retina, the energy in visual spectrum is converted into electrical potentials by rods and cones of retina through some chemical reactions.Impulses from rods and cones reach the cerebral cortex through optics nerve and the sensation of vision is produced in cerebral cortex Retina contains the visual receptors, which are also called photoreceptors or electromagnetic receptors. Visual receptors are rods and cones They are responsible for colour vision and perception of sharp, bright images.

PHYSIOLOGY OF VISION IN AYRUVEDA

In Ayurveda physiology of vision is based on the functions of Vata and Pitta. Light (Prakasha) is having Sookshma Guna, due to Sookshma Guna of Prakasha it reach till the photo receptors in retina traversing various layers. Chala Guna of Vata is responsible for photochemical activity in retina. Electrons are in a state of motion due to Chala Guna of Vata. When light falls on electrons, their intensity of motions increases. Due to Ushna Guna of Prakasha and Pitta along with Chala Guna of Vata is responsible in altering Sringhataka, represents the central controls .

KAPHA

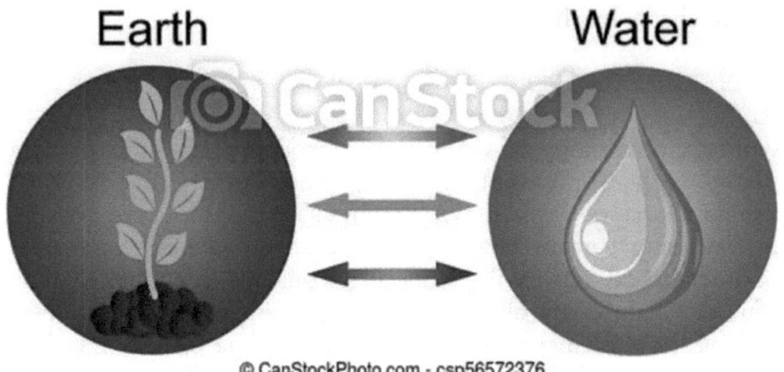

KAPHA DOSHA

स्नेहो बन्धः स्थिरत्वं च गौरवं वृषता बलम् । क्षमा धृतिरलोभश्चकफकर्माविकारजम् ।।*(च.सू. 18/53)*

Kapha Dosha – one of the three humours has the composition of earth and water. It provides structure and robustness to all things, it gives the cohesiveness needed to maintain a particular shape. It has properties of Lubricating the joints, hydrates and strengthens them, lot of energy and immunity to the body with compassionate, patient, loving personality.

प्रकृतस्तुबलंश्लेष्माविकृतोमलउच्यते,

सचैवोजःस्मृतःकायेसचपात्मोपदिश्यते (च. सू.17/115)

From the above Shloka of acharya charak it is very much clear that when this kapha Dosha is in its natural balanced form it has the potential of OJAS- strengthening the body.

त्रिविधं बलमिति-सहजं, कालजं युक्तिकृतं च । तत्र सहजं यच्छरीरसत्वयोः प्राकृतं, कालकृतमृतुविभागजं

वयस्कृतं च, युक्तिकृतं पुनस्तद्यदाहारचेष्टायोगजम्। च० सू० 11/34

Even Bal is ascribed to be of three types just like. Immunity Sahaj Balam means the natural immunity or the inborn immunity whereas Kalaj Balam implies Acquired immunity and Yuktikrit Balam is Artificial immunity.

Since the description Kapha Dosha in all texts of Ayurveda is in form of Bala- that is Strength- oja or immunity Hence we conclude and understand that the third of the Tridosha, is immune system of modern science.

To understand this in further details and in a more simpler manner lets now discuss the subtypes of kapha Dosha.

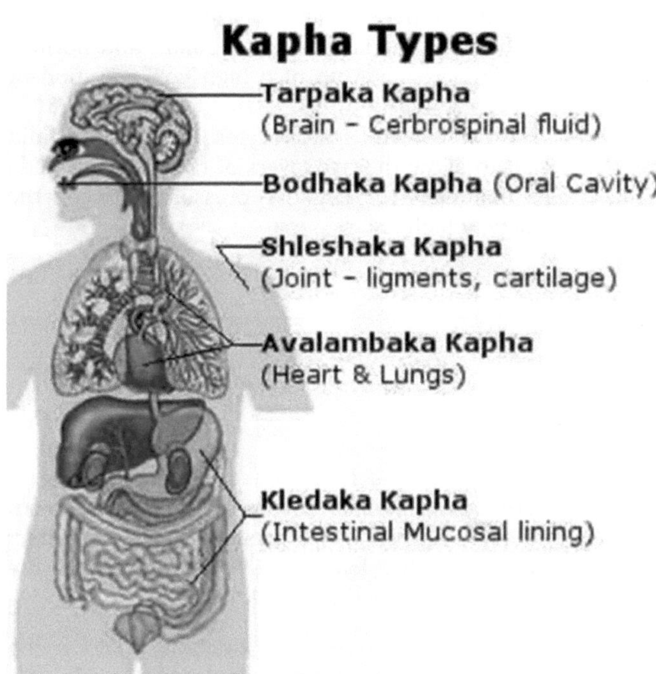

AVALAMBAKA KAPHA

उरःस्थस्त्रिकसन्धारणमात्मवीर्येणान्नरससहितेन हृदया करोति (सु.सू.

21/13)

The position of this Avlambak Kapha (pericardial, fluid surfactant,pleural fluid) is in the chest. It protects Trika and heart through it's ambukaram. Trika at chest region is a junction between sternum and clavicles - which is the location of thymus gland. "Ambu" means water - so the ambukaram of Avalambaka kapha indicates the lymphatic drainage. This Lymphatic drainage protects the body from microbes/ antigens, so the Avalambaka kapha is managing the local lymphoid nodes and Lymphatic drainage system of immune response to any antigens/microbes coming to this part. Pulmonary surfactant is a mixture of lipids and proteins which is secreted by the epithelial type II cells into the alveolar space.It is established that pulmonary surfactant reduces surface tension at the air–water interface in the alveoli,thereby preventing collapse of these structures at end expiration In pericardial fluid from higher to lower concentration being albumin, globulins,macroglobulins, and fibrinogen are present. The fluid is made up of a high concentration of lactate

dehydrogenase (LDH), protein and lymphocytes. The pleural fluid functions as a lubricant to allow the two layers of the pleura to glide smoothly and it also maintains the negative pressure between the lungs and thoracic cavity, which is

KLEDAKA KAPHA

यस्त्वामाशयसंस्थितः क्लेदकः । सोऽन्नसंघातक्लेदनात् ।।

अ० हृ० सू० 12/13

The seat of this kapha is stomach. It's function is moistening of food. The mucus secretions of stomach protects the stomach from foreign toxins or microbes. The HCL also provides innate immunity and the GALT - Gut associated Lymphoid tissue present in the Stomach may also be considered as the Kledak kapha.

MODERN ASPECTS OF KLEDAKA KARMA OF KAPHA-the food that we eat undergoes mastication process by teeth and

thoroughly mixed with saliva. The primary function of saliva helps in lubrication, swallowing, appreciation of taste and facilitates speech.The principal glands of salivation are the parotid, submandibular, and sublingual glands; in addition, there are many very small buccal glands. Daily secretion of saliva normally ranges between 800 and

1500 milliliters, the average value of 1000 milliliters. Saliva contains two types of protein secretion: (1) a serous secretion that contains ptyalin (an α-amylase), which is an enzyme for digesting starches, and(2) mucus secretion that contains mucin for lubricating and for surface protective purposes. saliva also helps for the deglutition of food taken through the oral cavity by forming a bolus of food. The bolus of food enters the esophagus and reaches to stomach through

esophagus.

As the bolus reaches to Amashaya, it undergoes the first stage of paaka known as madhura awasthaa paka during which kapha is produced which is like froth in nature. If we compare this stage with the modern science, it

appears that carbohydrates, fat, and protein of diet are first digested by saliva and gastric secretions.

BODHAK KAPHA:

रसबोधनात् बोधको रसनास्थायी ।

अ० हृ० सू० 12/17

The site of this Kapha is buccal cavity. It helps in perception of taste. Salivary gland secretions not only lubricates the food but also provides protection to buccal cavity from microbes and antigens to certain extent. The Lymphoid Tissue in buccal cavity is tonsillar tissue. So the Bodhak kapha represents salivary glands secretions as well as tonsils.Lymphoid tissue. Bodhaka is located at the root of tongue and throat, it helps in the perception of taste because of the gustatory sense organ being watery in nature. According to modern science, taste is a chemical sensation. Saliva by
its solvent action dissolves the solid food substances, so that the dissolved substances can stimulate the taste buds.
The stimulated taste buds recognize the taste. Taste is impaired when the mouth is dry, because substances can only
be tasted when in solution.

Rasa Bodhana- Perception of Taste
Taste is a chemical sensation. Unless substance is in solution, taste buds can be stimulated. Saliva dissolves the solid food substances, by its solvent action. So that the dissolved substances stimulate the taste buds by acting on microvilli of taste receptors exposed into the papillae. Stimulated taste buds recognize the taste, so here saliva is acting as an instruct-

or for perception of taste. This is nothing but the function of Bodhaka Kapha.

· Bodhaka Kapha- Digestion

Saliva will aid in the process of digestion by moistening and softening the food in oral cavity and allowing the enzymatic activity to take place. In oral cavity the action of salivary amylase and lingual lipase as a part of chemical digestion is assisted by the saliva. In the mechanical digestion also it has its own role in the process of mastication which is manipulated by the tongue. So Kapha which is present in the oral cavity or the saliva which does the Kledana / softening of the food can be correlated with Bodhaka Kapha.

TARPAK KAPHA :

शिरःसंस्थोऽर्पणात् तर्पकः [अ.द.सू.12/17]

Situated in the head, functions to protect the sense organs. The Tarpak kapha is represented by CSF, Glial cells and microglia which protects the head. Tarpaka Kapha can be related to the functions of Cerebrospinal fluid which is responsible for the nourishment of different centres of the brain which control sense organs, fluid in eye, ear, nose, tongue which is responsible for the nourishment of receptors in respective sense organ.

Tarpaka Kapha is said to be nourishment of Indriya (senseorgans/controlling sense organs).

SHLESHAK KAPHA:

संधिसंश्लेषात् श्लेषकः संधिषु स्थितः ।।

अ० हु० शा० 12/17

This Kapha is present in the joints and functions for their Lubrication and easy and smooth movements. The fluid protects joints at the time of its movements and in autoimmune conditions like SLE .The role played by synovial fluid is same to that of shleshak This Kapha, which is located in all the bony joints keep them strongly or firmly united, protects their articulation and prevents disunion.Synovial fluid contains lubricin (glycoprotein),secreted by synovial fibroblasts. . There also is some evidence that it helps regulate synovial cell growth.

Kapha dosha is immune system

In equilibrium state kapha promotes strength that is why normal kapha is called ojas. Hence it is the master of the human immune system. Functions of normal kapha are like that of ojas. Kapha supports the body by performing functions like binding of joints, unction, healing, saturation, giving strength and stability to the body The normal functions of kapha are unctuousness, cohesion, firmness, heaviness, potency, strength, forbearance, patience and absence of greed all these factors help in strengthning the body both physically as well as mentally.

The word immunity means the state of protection from infectious disease. The immune system evolved as defense system to protect body from microorganisms Ayurvedic system of medicine not only deals with treating the diseases but also aims to prevention the disease. Vyadhikshamatva (Immunity) is described in Ayurveda and this concept is considered equivalent to immunity.

Vyadhikshamatva

In Sanskrita, the word Vyadhikshamatva" is made up of two words; Vyadhi (disease) and Kshamatva (suppress or overcome).According to Ayurveda, Vyadhi is conditions which come into existence as consequence of in-equilibrium between Doshas ,Dhatus (tissues systems) and Malas. These factors, in their normal status are responsible in maintaining the physical and psychological health. The word, Kshamatva" is derived from,„Kshamus sahane" which means to be patient or composed to suppress anger, to keep quite or to resist. Therefore Vyadhikshamatwa means the factor which limits the pathogenesis and opposes the strength of disease.

Chakrapani Datta, while commenting on Charaka Samhita, gave his view on the term Vyadhikshamatva

(I) Vyadhi-balavirodhitvam: It is the capacity to restrain or withstand the strength (severity) of the diseases i.e. strength to resist the progress of disease.

(II) Vyadhi-utpadakapratibandhakatva: The resisting power of the body competent enough to prevent the occurrence and re-occurrence of the disease.

These sub-types of Vyadhikshamatva commutatively form the resistance which now a day known as Immunity.

According to ayurveda the balanced kapha is regarded as bala(strength/immunity)

Type of Bala and their correlation with conventional medical science

Immune system is one of the most important system of the body. The defence mechanism attributed against Pathogenic micro-organisms, toxins and other antigens helps, protects the body from being diseased and helps to lead healthy life. The Immune system comprises of innate immune system and adaptive immune system. The texts of Ayurveda depicts the normal balanced kapha Dosha as Bala or ojas which is of three types. Sahaj, Kalaj, Yuktikrit.

Sahaj bala

The Sahaj bala of Ayurveda has properties similar to innate immunity of Modern In this there is rapid triggering of inflammatory responses based on the recognition of either molecules expressed by microorganisms that serve as "danger signals" released by cells under attack These receptors / ligand interactions trigger signalling events that ultimately lead to inflammation.

Kalaja bala

(It depends on the Factors like Age and Climatic Conditions.)

1. Kaalatah Bala (Bala differing as per seasons or climate)

   There is a study showing that the activity

   Uttama in Hemanta and Shishira ritu

   Madhyama in Vasanta Sharada

   Heena in Grishma varsha

1. seasonality also affects our immune

   Almost a quarter of our genes differs according to the time of year, some are more active in winter and others in summer.

3.Researches prove that Physiological Ageing is accompanied by decline in immune system function .

- Elderly are reportedly more prone to various chronic and infectious diseases as compared with youth.

1. Vaya Bala

(Bala with reference to Age groups)

Uttama bala ------Youvana (upto 30years)

Madhyama bala ---- (30-60 Years)

Heena bala-----Vruddha (above 60 years)

Yuktikrit bala

The word yukti means planning. It can be named as adaptive immunity. This adaptive immune system is based on clonal recognition of antigens followed by antigen reactive cells and execution of an immune effector program.

When the entire tissues, starting from Rasadhatu to Shukradhatu are in a fully nourished state and energy is derived from them to perform all types of physical and mental activities, that state is known as bala that is bodily energy / immunity.

Vyadhishamatva /immunity is widely explained in Ayurveda as the main Basic focus of Ayurveda is

"SwasthasyaSwasthysRakshnam, Aaaturasyavikaarprashmanam"

In modern aspect the immune systems in general working is- clearance of antigen by immune complex formation between antigen, complement and antibody - this pattern is in corelation to ayurvedic Dosha -Dushya - Samurchana of [disturbed Dosha invade tissues and affect whole body in gradations]

Innate, or nonspecific, immunity is the defense system with which we are born. It protects us against all antigens. Innate immunity involves barriers that keep harmful materials from entering our body. These barriers form the first line of defense in the immune response. it also comes in a protein chemical form, called innate humoral immunity. Examples include the body's complement system and substances called interferon and interleukin-1 (which causes fever).If an antigen gets past these barriers, it is attacked and destroyed by other parts of the immune system.

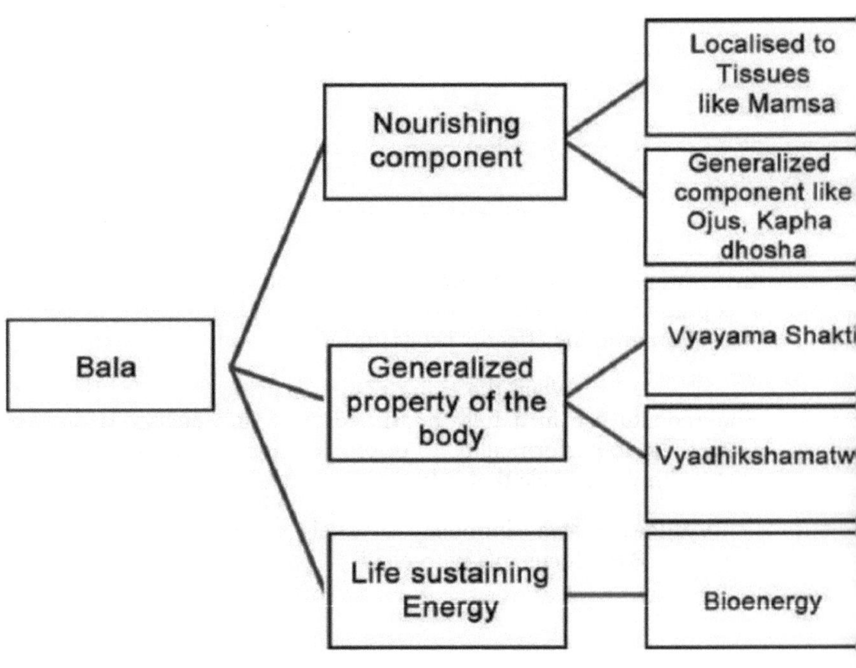

ACQUIRED IMMUNITY

Acquired immunity is immunity that develops with exposure to various antigens. our immune system builds a defense against that specific antigen.

PASSIVE IMMUNITY

Passive immunity is due to antibodies that are produced in a body other than our own. Infants have passive immunity because they are born with antibodies that are transferred through the placenta from their mother. These antibodies disappear between ages 6 to 12 months.

Passive immunization may also be due to injection of antiserum, which contains antibodies that are formed by another person or animal. It provides immediate protection against an antigen, but does not provide long-lasting protection. Immune serum globulin (given for hepatitis exposure) and tetanus antitoxin are examples of passive immunization.

The immune system includes certain types of white blood cells. It also includes chemicals and proteins in the blood, such as antibodies, complement proteins, and interferon. Some of these directly attack foreign substances in the body, and others work together to help the immune system cells.

Lymphocytes are a type of white blood cell. There are B and T type lymphocytes.

- B lymphocytes become cells that produce antibodies. Antibodies attach to a specific antigen and make it easier for the immune cells to destroy the antigen.
- T lymphocytes attack antigens directly and help control the immune response. They also release chemicals, known as cytokines, which control the entire immune response.

As lymphocytes develop, they normally learn to tell the difference between our own body tissues and substances that are not normally found in our body. Once B cells and T cells are formed, a few of those cells will multiply and provide "memory" for our immune system. This allows our immune system to respond faster and more efficiently the next time we are exposed to the same antigen. In many cases, it will prevent us from getting sick.

4. SAPTA DHATU

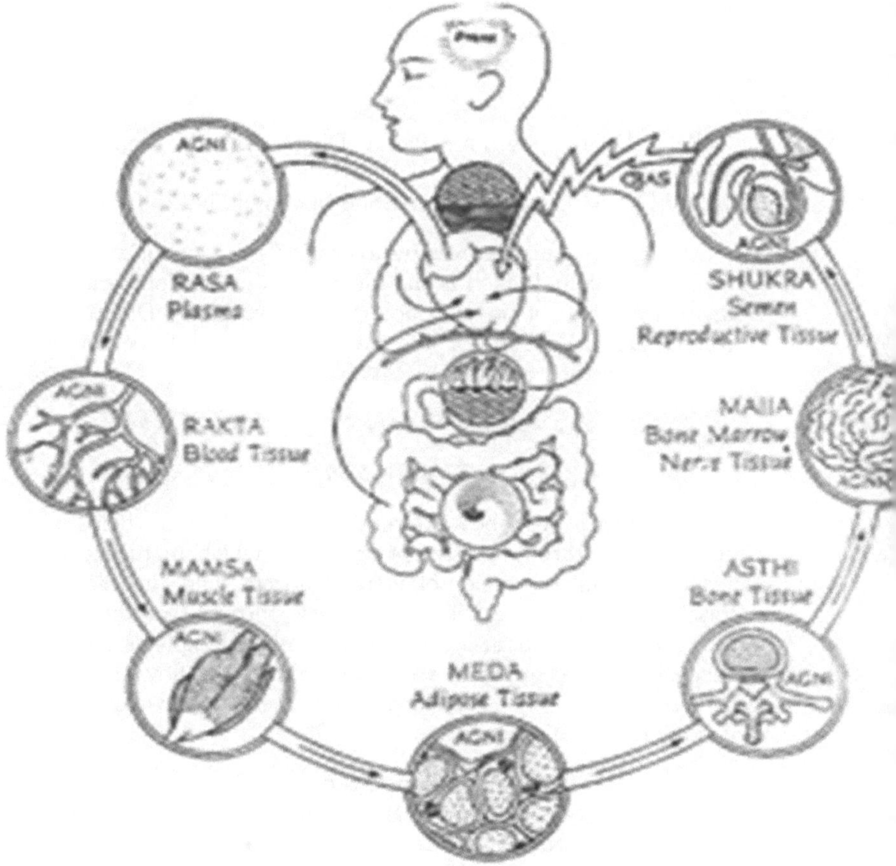

RASA
Plasma

RAKTA
Blood Tissue

MAMSA
Muscle Tissue

MEDA
Adipose Tissue

ASTHI
Bone Tissue

MAJJA
Bone Marrow,
Nerve Tissue

SHUKRA
Semen
Reproductive Tissue

OJAS

AGNI

DHATU

Dhatus are the structural unit of Body

"Dhaarnaath Dhaatven"

The one who supports and "nourishes" itself and other Dhatus according to Ayurveda. Dhatus undergo continous construction and degeneration to maintain a state of equillibrium of the body. In ayurveda the Dhatus formation depends on the nourishment we specieve in the from of food material (Ahama) This Ahora is worked upon by Jathragani. to transform into Ahara Ras and kitta (waste Products) The functions of Ahara Rasa is Tarpan (Nourishment) Vardhan (to increase-grow) Dharan[Support) yapan [to be useful in future] This Aahar Rasa undergoes transformation by the action of Bhutagnis [Panchmahabhutagniz] and Dhatwagnis respectively for the formation of Dhatus in the Following chronological order :

Rasa Dhatu [Plasma], Rakta Dhatu [Blood] Mamsa Dhatu {Muscular Tissue] Meda Dhatu{Adipose Tissue/Red Bone Marrow] Majja Dhatu [Yellow Bone Marrow] Shukra Dhatu

During formation of dhatus there is formation of sthai dhatu and poshak dhatu.[which is the factor for the development of next Dhatu following it in chronology, as Precursor Dhatu] Three NAYAY are described for the nourishment and Development of Dhatus from their precursors..

Kedari Kulya Nayaya- Theory of channels and fields.

सारस्तु सप्तभिर्भूयो यथास्वं पच्यतेऽग्निभिः ।। अ० ३० शा० 3/61

This theory describes different tissues as different fields, which receive water through different channels, which in turn are connected to a big reserveior of water Nutrient fluid in this case is "Rasa" which nourishes all other tissues , through specific channels meant for Specific tissues. this theory probably explains the importance of pressure gradient, which determines the flow of fluid into the tissue spaces This is similar to the movement of water in the direction of gravitational force

This theory can also explain the passive diffusion of particles across the cell membrane, along the concentration gradient as occurs in case use of co_2,o, etc.

KHALE KAPOTA NYAYA-THEORY OF GRAINS

This theory explains the autoregulation of blood. flow by tissue factors. Blood flow to each tissue is regulated depending on the metabolic needs of the particular tissue. The example given for this theory. is that of different pigeons, picking up the grains. from the same field and then returning to their original places Here, the choice regarding the amount of grains purely depends on the individual pigeons need

This theory can also explain the transport of different particles across the cell-membrane with the expenditure of energy as occurs in case of different molecules like glucose, amino acids and Some ions. This is. because, the pigeons in the above example have to spend energy. to procure the grains and this process is "active "one" and the term "pigeons" denotes Dhatus where as "Khale" is the Aahar Ras [Nutrients]

KSIRA - DADHI-NYAYA -Theory of milk & curd

This theory speaks of one tissue into another in a particular order through the activity of respective "Dhatvagni." The example given to state this theory is that of transformation of milk into curd, curd into butter and butter into ghee in particular order

This theory can be explained at molecular level. All metabolic pathways like glycolytic pathway. Krebs TCA cycle, B-oxidation pathway, Urea cycle, Gluconeogenesis etc could be the examples for this type of transformations with the involvement of their specific enzymes.

Ek-KALA DHATU PUTAN NYAYA -Theory of simultaneous process

Arundutta has described that the aahar rasa percolates into all the dhatuvaha srotas simultaneously This theory is known as ek dhatu poshana paksha The aahar rasa circulates in whole body continuously for all times by normal activity of vyan vayu since charak explains the formation of dhatu from Ahara Rasa is a cyclic and continuous process. Rasa is circulated all over the body by vyan vayu and nourishes all the Dhatus so, EK-kala-Dhatu Poshan nyaya ard means that Dhatus get their nourishment Simultaneously through different processes like kshira dadhi nyaya , khale Kapota nyaya, Kedari kulya nyaya.

So its concluded that the classical concept of nyaya is equivalent to different physiological processes described in metabolic transformations of food.

SAPT DHATU THEORY

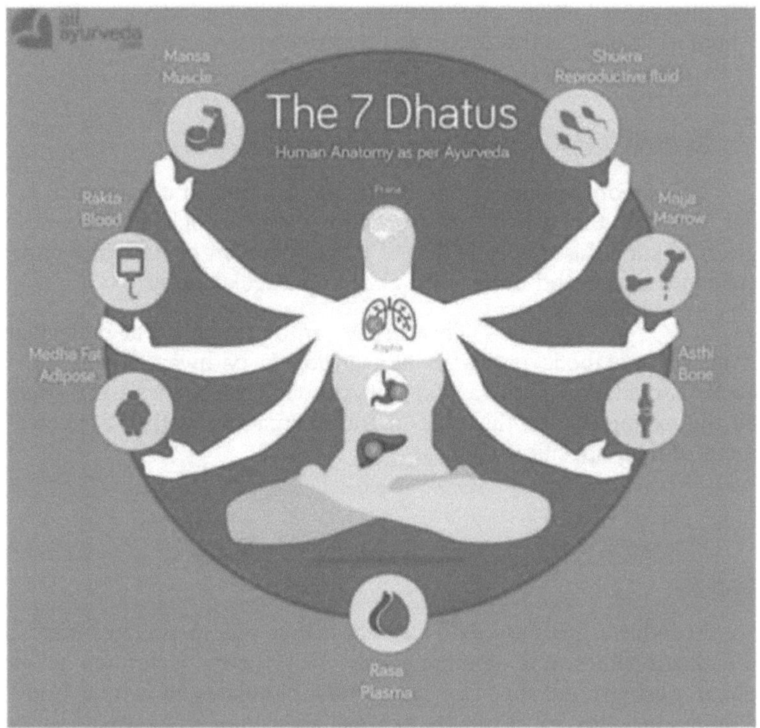

The term Dhatu highlights all the basic elements which render three main functions - nutrition - Sustenance and growth in general.

रसासृङ्मांसमेदोऽस्थिमज्जाशुक्राणिच्यातव:

Ras, Rakta, Mamsa, Meda, Asthi, Majja, Shukra are the Seven Dhatus according to Ayurveda. Although this classification of saptdhatu is not under any histological Study but still it's very clear that even at ancient time the concept of tissue was very much prevailing. This Ras dhatu of ayurveda has properties similar to plasma and Lymph [intravascular fluid] whereas the Rakt Dhatu is symbolic to blood of modern science Mamsa Dhatu is none other than the muscular tissue. Medo dhatu is ofcourse the adipose tissue and circulating lipids as its been divided into two forms Badha and Abadha. Majja is nothing but filling of bony cavities there by representing the modern bone marrow tissue where as shukra dha

tu stands for all hormones of hypothalamo-pituitary gonadal axis and sperm-ova. Now to understand these sapt dhatus in more simpler form let us focus on what acharyas say about each.

Ras Dhatu:

The word rasa means sap, juice, or liquid. In the physical body, rasa refers directly to the plasma, or non cellular portion of the blood; the lymph, and interstitial fluids. As watery secretions, rasa dhatu relates indirectly to breast milk and menstrual fluid. Rasa is more than fluid, it is nourishmentThe main function of Rasdhatu is "PRINAN" which means providing nutrition if we minutely try to understand we will know that Rasdhatu is Jal mahabhut pradhaan, so its in fluid form chronologically ayurveda has put this Dhatu at number one.

1 . It is formed as a result of digestion of food.

2. It flows throughout the body.

All these above mentioned properties of Ras Dhatu are in accordance to blood component - Plasma which carries nutrients. From modern point of view plasma content in blood is 55% and it contains-water, Salts, enzymes, antibodies, proteins, the most important function of plasma is to transport nutritions throughout the body, transport wastes and maintains blood volume, body immunity and electrolyte balance and functions of Ras dhatu corelate to plasma.The health of one main bodily tissue, i.e Rasa dhatu is responsible for the quality and health of all other tissues. Rasa dhatu is the plasma or the circulatory fluid present in the blood that provides development support and nutrition to blood cells, muscles, fat, bone, bone marrow and our sexual & reproductive fluids.

Hridya (heart) is the seat of rasa dhatu from the heart it travels through the twenty-four dhamnis, ten of them going

upwards, ten going downwards and four going side wards obliquely. By travelling all along the body it provides the proper nourishment to the body and gives proper support to the body. It does the following functions i.e.,

- it nourishes the entire body constantly (tarpayati)
- make it grow(vardhyati),
- supports(dharyati),
- maintains the living (yapyati).

Ahara rasa is formed from ahara after action of jatharagni. Saman Vayu brings the absorbed ahara rasa to hridya thus control the venous return. Vyaan vayu ejects the rasa from the ventricle of the heart with appropriate pressure. The rasadhatu then circulates in the whole body always, continuously and simultaneously. From hridya with the help of vyan vayu through all dhamni sirasa is reached to small arteries, arterioles, and capillaries and make it available to the level of all dhatus and provide nourishment. Thus,

TARPYATI

Rasa dhatu helps to nourish dhatus in every stage of life beginning from balyawastha, madhyawastha and up to vriddhawastha as well (till the end of this life). Rasadhatu is very important for maintenance of normal functions and to provide energy so as to make the one alive and kicking. Rasadhatu helps in transportation of proper nutrients from one tissue to another.

VARDHYATI

Rasa dhatu helps in growth of dhatus during balyawastha because it carries growth hormone. In the first phase of life for the organogenesis and the dhatuvriddhi, the nutrients for the development and growing of these are very important. Rasa dhatu

provides proper nourishment to all dhatu and updhatu in the balya phase, so as the body properly grow.

DHARYATI

Middle stage of life is yuvawasta and it is the most important avastha in one's life. One is supposed to be as fit as fiddle in this

stage because of complete development of tissues and organ in this stage. So, in this stage dosha, dhatu and mala becomes more

stable. This action comes under dharana karma of rasadhatu.Some acharyas have referred both word dharana and Jeevan are

synonym. In this stage swaroop of sharir should remain in its

original and proper shape which is only possible due to rasa.

YAPYATI

Due to paripakvata of sharir in vriddhawastha, annarasa does only little nourishment in this awastha so as only required for maintenance of life. This is called yapan karma. During the vriddhawastha all the dhatu gets ksheena. Ageing cause decrease

in dhatu, updhatu, dosha and mala due to the degeneration of body tissues. In spite of degeneration of cells, rasadhatu helps to

maintain the life and prevent the body from total destruction. This is called the yapanakarma.

A close look at the functions of rasa dhatu and plasma make it clear that ras dhatu is none other than the plasma of modern science.

स (रस) शब्दार्थिर्जलसन्तानवदनादिशेषेणानुधावत्येवशरीरेकेवलम्

- *रसाद्रक्तंप्रजायते (च.वि. 15/15)*
- *रसस्तुष्टिं प्राणनं रक्तपुष्टिं च करोति ।।*
  सु० सू० 15/6

RAKTA DHATU

तेजोरसानांसर्वेषांमनुजाना'भकुच्यतेपित्तोष्मणसरागेणरसोरक्तत्वमृच्छति (च .चिः 15/27)

Ras Dhatu is acted upon by Ranjak Pitta In pleeha and Yakrit and the biochemical action of this pitta imparts red colouration along with many which are owing to the action of agni (Ranjak

Pitta).The main function of rakta dhatu is delineated as "jivana" which means the indication and sustenance of vitality. prana vayu from the external atmosphere is transformed into its bodily assumable form and then circulated with the blood into the whole body there by performing its function of jivana.
According to sushruta and charaka raktadhatu is must for living body. it's answerable for giving support, for promotion of strength, complexion, and happiness, nutrition to the succeeding dhatu and long life to the body .

We know in modern perspective RBC's are the Red Blood cells of blood its due to these cells that the colour of blood is considered red. These RBC's formation takes place in Liver in foetal life and in spleen, bone marrow in adult life. These RBC's formation Site co-related to Ayurvedic site of Ranjak Pitta and Ranjan of Rasdhatu.

Now let's further evaluate the fact that Acharyas have accepted red colour of RaktDhatu but none of them comes out with a single red colour definition. They have compared the red colour of RaktDhatu with different examples.

तपनीयेन्द्रगोपाभं पदमालक्तकसन्निभम् ।

गुंजाफलसवर्ण च विशुद्धं विद्धि शोणितम् ।। (च.सू. 24/22)

इन्द्रगोपप्रतीकाशमसंहतं आविवर्णं च प्रकृतिस्थं जानीयात् ।(सु.सू. 14/22)

मधुरं लवणं किंचिद् शीतोष्णमसंहतम्।

पद्मेन्द्रगोपहेमाविशशलोहितलोहितम् ।। (अ.हृ.सू. 27 / 1)

That means it is very clear that the red colour of RaktDhatu has variation in its redness. Same is agreed at modern science level. They also say the Bloods red colour will depend on the percentage of Haemoglobin presence, which imparts the red colour to RBCs. Now let us take a look at the Panchtbhautik Swarup of RaktaDhatu

विस्त्रता द्रवता रागश्चलनं विलयस्तथा ।

भूम्यादिपंचमूतानामेते रक्तगुणाः स्मृताः । (शा.उ.12/4)

According to Ayurveda Rakt Datu has visra smell, its liquid, Red in colour, has pulsation and is light. Same characteristics of blood are mentioned in modern science which says that blood has metallic smell, its red coloured liquid, it's pulsation can be felt in arteries.

Now further to relate the functions of Blood to that of Raktdhatu

रक्तं सर्वशरीरस्थं जीवस्याधारमुत्तमम् ॥ (शा.उ. 6/9)

तद्धविशुद्धं हि रुधिरं वलवर्णसुखायुषाः ।

युनक्ति प्राणिनं प्राणाः शोणितं ह्यनुवर्तते । (च.सू. 24/4)

From the above shlokas it's clear that Raktdhatu moves in the whole body and is the cause of praan/jivan to the body. Now let's understand its function in respect of modern perspective. According to modern theory blood flows throughout the body (raktsarvsharirshth) and provides oxygen, (Praan) along with other nutrients to each and every cell of the body(जीवनं)

Pramaan of RaktaDhatu:

It has got eight anjaliPramaan according to Ayurveds. Now this eight anjali is more than 1.5 litres. According to Modern science the average of total volume of blood in a human body is 4.5 to 5 litres out of which 3 litres is plasma(RasDhatu) so the Serum [Blood/RaktaDhatu] is 1.5 – 2 liters depending on person to person

Signs of Normal blood volume in body

प्रसन्नवर्णेन्द्रियमिन्द्रियार्थानिच्छन्ततमव्याहतपक्तृवेगम्।

सुखान्वितं पुष्टिबलोपपन्नं विशुद्धरक्तं पुरुषं वदन्ति । (च.सू. 24/24)

According to ayurveda the one who has RaktDhatu in appropriate pramaan will be a happy person with energy and enthusiasm for work, the modern view also holds the same signs of proper haemoglobin concentration in the body.If the RaktDhatu is increased from its usual pramaan

following symptoms will appear according to acharyas -

- Redness in Eyes
- Veins prominence
- High B.P.
- sleepy
- Inflammed body
- Itching
- Malesma
- Loss of appetite
- Joints pain
- Skin problems

All these above mentioned Ayurvedic approach for increased RaktDhatu symptoms are exactly in line to the increased haemoglobin symptoms.

RaktDhatukshay

The dryness and hardness of skin, it becomes Lusterless, unconsciousness, desire to have sweet & sour food, headache.XWell in modern perspective the correlation is with anaemia - where fatigue, nausea, headache, Lusterters skin [Paleness], chest pain, dizziness Shortness of breath, weakness are the symptoms. if we try to co relate the Modern &Ayurvedic Symptoms we can easily say that they almost relate to each other

Mamsa Dhatu

Mamsa Dhatu is the third dhatu in chronology of Saptadhatu. It's main functions are lepan and sharirpushti. It is the main cementing, bonding component of the body, holding the body, limbs and organs together. It maintains Physical strength of the body. It is Prithvi Mahabhuta Pradhaan Dhatu.Acharya charak considers,Peshi number to be 400 whereasSushrut says the number is 500. Mansa Dhatu is in forms of groups in the body .these groups are called muscles,/ pesh

मांसावयवसंघातः परस्परं विभक्तः पेशीत्युच्यते ॥

According to Ayurveda Muscles (Peshi) may be large in Size ,small, thick, thin, flat, round, firm, soft, Smooth, rough and their functions are mentioned in the following shloka:

सिरास्नाय्वस्थिमर्माणि संधयश्च शरीरिणाम्।

पेशिभिः संवृतान्यत्र बलवंति भवंत्यतः ॥ (सु.शा. 5/38

Peshi covers and protects all the siraas, Joints, bones and provides strength & them and body, similarly in modern science the functions of muscular system are support, protection Movement in accordance to the functions of Peshi.Now let's have a close look at *Mamsa Vriddhi symptopms*

मांस स्फिगण्डौष्ठोपस्थोरुबाहुजंघासु वृद्धिं गुरुगात्रतां च । (सु.सू. 15/14)

If muscles mass increases in body there is extra muscle volume at waist, lips, chest, arms, thigh. Same is mentioned under the modern view of obesity.

Mamsakshaya Lakshan

मांसक्षये विशेषेण स्फिग्ग्रीवोदरशुष्कता । (च.सू. 17/65)

If Mamsa Dhatukshaya occurs there is loss of muscle volume is neck, abdomen etc. basically what's mentioned here is the chief symptoms to access the kshaya , these sites are the ones where predominantly an increase or decrease in the volume of Mansa is observed. So Acharyas have taken these sites as criteria To conclude kshayas, though once the kshaya takes place there are lot many other changes in addition to the above mentioned ones

Mamsa dhatu is very essential Dhatu in body which is responsible for manifestation of proper nourishment it is responsible for the strength, stamina and power of body. Mamsa Dhatu can be compared to Muscular tissue in modern science but Ayurvedic texts reveal that Mamsa Dhatu has much broader concept than Muscular tissue. It maintains the metabolism of Vasa (Omentum) andTvacha (skin and its layers) as its Updhatu(Accessory tissue) and Kha Malaas its excretory product. The well build musculature of a person indicates good and proper nourishment of the individual. This excellence of Mamsa Dhatu seen in such a person is resembled by Mamsa Sara Purusha with its specific symptoms.

Medo Dhatu

स्वोष्मणा पक्वमेव तत् ।

स्वतेजोऽम्बुगुणस्निग्धोद्रिक्तं मेदोऽभिजायते ।। च० चि० 15/28

According to the above shloka Mamsa Dhatu with increase in it's Tej (Agnis) and Jala guna undergoes paak and there is formation of Meda Dhatu.To understand Medo Dhatu from a modern perspective, it can be said that there are 2 types of MedoDhatu

1. Baddha Meda or Poshya Medo Dhatu.
2. Abaddha Meda or Poshaka Medo Dhatu.

1. Poshya / Baddha Medo DhatuPoshya Medo Dhatu is stored in Medodharakala. It is immobile in nature (Gativivarjita). Udara and
Anuasthi are sites of Medodhaarakala. Other sites like Sphikka, Stana and Gala are also depots of Poshya Meda.

2. Poshaka/ Abaddha Meda DhatuPoshaka Medo Dhatu is mobile (gatiyukta) and circulated with Rasa-Rakta Dhatu in the whole body to provide nutrition to Poshya MedoDhatu. Circulating lipids along with cholesterol within the blood can be visualised by different imaging techniques. After Mamsagnipaka, this Poshaka MedoDhatu is distinguished in the form of Sukshmabhaga &
Sthulabhaga and then further transformation of MedoDhatu occurs by this.

Functions of Medo Dhatu

मेदः स्नेहस्वेदौ दृढत्वं पुष्टिमस्थ्नां च । (सु.सू. 15/5)

1) SnehanaLustre of skin, hair and eyes depends upon Sneha quality of Meda. In Medovridhhi or Medoroga, the Snigdhagatrata arises which may be due to Snehana function of Meda.

2) Sweda
Sweda is mala of Medo Dhatu. Acharya Sharangdhara listed Sweda as Upadhatu of meda.

3) AsthipushtiNourishment of further Dhatu i.e., Asthi Dhatu is also a function of Medo Dhatu. Nourishment of its snayu upadhatu, (and Sandhi acc. to Chakrapani), is another function of medodhatu.

4) DridhatvaDridhatva or strength is provided by snayu upadhatu of

meda. Layers of fatty tissue depots over the underlying organ present in the abdomen protect from outside pressure and frictions. Dridhatva is also taken as energy as meda is an energy store of the body and provides almost double energy compared to carbohydrates and proteins.

5) Netra and Gatrasnigdhta both are a symptom of Sthaulya and may produce due to increase Snehana function of Meda.

AcharyaSushruta and Acharya Vagbhatta mentioned kati and mamsa as the second moola of medovah sortas which seems less physiologically and more anatomically correct as compared to vapavahan which is mentioned by Acharya Charak as the second moola of medovahsrotas.

VRIKKA

Vrikka is formed from Sara part of Rakta(blood) and Meda (fat). Its function is to nourish the meda. The situation of vrikka, which are 2 in number, is in both the side of the mid vertebral line inside the abdominal cavity. According to Acharya Sharangdhara, vrikka nourishes the medo Dhatu inside the stomach area of the abdominal cavity19 while Acharya Charak mentioned them as Moola of Medovah Srotas. Acharya Sushruta and Vagabhatta also mentioned Vrikka as the Moola of Medovah srotas and also placed at the primary position. There is no clear evidence of kidneys taking part in fat metabolism both according to modern science and Ayurveda. But if suprarenal glands, which are present just above the kidney attached to it, and function in the body in the metabolism of fat by its secretions, the perspective of Acharyas can be correctly established with correct relation according to modern science. Hence vrikka (kidney) with suprarenal glands are Moola of Medovah Srotas.

VAPAVAHAN

Acharya Chakrapani also accepted the viewpoint of Acharya Charak of Vapavahan as the place of meda.

It is also known as Taila vartika. Dr.Ghanekar explained it as the place where maximum meda is stored The location of vapavahan is beneath the Jathare (stomach) and beyond Pleeha (spleen). Kloma is also used as the synonym of vapavahan.Kloma in ayurvedic science is not clearly defined. But it is included in kosthanga according to Acharya Charak. So, based on this fact, if pancreas is kloma, which is very important for digestion and metabolism of fat, the vapavahan can be called the moola of medovaha srotas. Physiologically the fact fits in both Ayurveda and Modern science's perspective.

KATI

Kati is the place where generally the fat accumulates.Kati is mentioned as Moola by Acharya Sushruta. Anatomically kati has a big amount of fat around it, and in patients with obesity, it is vast in quantity.This may be the reason why Acharya Sushruta mentioned kati as the Medovaha srotas moola.

MAMSA

The layer of fat under the skin is closely related to the muscles. Mamsa as Medovah srotasmoola can be correlated with the vasa (mamsagata sneha) below the skin. That's why Acharya Vagabhatta considered Mamsa as Mola of Medovah srotas.

The Very recent researches on the origin of adipose tissue have found the ability of myogenic cells to differentiate toward adipogenic lineage i.e there are progenitors in myogenic cells for certain adipose tissue formation

स्थूलास्थिषु विशेषेण मज्जात्वाभ्यंतराशितः । अथतरेषु सर्वेषुसरक्तं मेद उच्यते ॥ (सु.शा. 4/13)

Acharya Sushrut has defined Meda Dhatu site –the one in abdomen and small bones. He mentioned its colour to be red. Now lets understand the adipose tissues functions. Adipose tissue is considered to be of two types

- The white coloured adipose tissue - which is present in the visceral organs and beneath skin as well as the central cavity of bones [Bone marrow)
- The brown adipose tissue which is Present during the foetal life.

The functions of both these forms of adipose tissues is - providing energy, heat, protection, strength to the body - Similar to Meda dhatu functions.

Medkshaya versus Lipodystrophy

संधीनां स्फूटनं ग्लानिरक्षणोरायास एव च।

लक्षणं मेदसि क्षीणे तनुत्वमुदरस्य च । (च.सू. 17/66)

Splitting like Joint pains, sensationg emptiness in eyes, feeling of exhaustion, sunken abdomen. almost same kind of symptoms are observed in Lipodystrophy.

MEDO VRIDDHI

तद्वन्मेदस्तथा श्रमम् ।

अल्पेऽपि चेष्टिते श्वासं स्फिक्स्तनोदरलम्बनम्॥ (अ.हृ.सू. 11/10)

In medovriddhi even slight exertion is not tolerated. There is breathlessness, hanging or protruding of buttocks, breast, abdomen.

Again all these signs are seen in excess adipose tissue accummulation in body.

ASTHI DHATU

Formation of Asthi Dhatu

पृथिव्यग्न्यनिलादीनां संघातः स्वोष्मणा कृतः ।

खरत्वं प्रकरोत्यस्य जायतेऽस्थि ततोनृणाम् ॥ (च.चि. 15/31)

The essential nutrients of Medo dhatu are digested and transformed by Asthi dhatwagni together with prithvi, Agni & vayu to form Asthi Dhatu.Many researches are going on and trying to conclude the role of bone marrow adipocytes in bone remodelling. These adipocytes are also regarded as osteoblasts - which have a chief role in bone formation and whose depleted number is cause of osteoporosis and other bone deformities

Types of Bones

एत ।निपंचविधानि भवन्ति । तद्यथा-कपालरुचकतरुणवलयनलकसंज्ञानि ।(सु.शा. 5/22)

AYURVEDIC VIEW	MODERN VIEW
KAPAL ASTHI	FLAT BONE
RUCHAKA ASTHI	TEETH
TARUNASTHI	CARTILAGE
VALAYA	CURVED BONES(RIBS)
NALAK	LONG BONES

Functions of Asthi Dhatu

According to Ayurvedic View Asthi dhatu :-

- Supports the body
- Nourishes majja Dhatu
- Supports Mamsa Dhatu
- Supports blood vessels & tendons.

It is also said that like a tree is supported strongly with compact mass and has branches so is a person supported by a strong bony skeleton.Gelling with these functions the modern view agrees to all these ones apart from many more being mentioned by them.

Asthi kshaya

अस्थिक्षयेऽस्थिशूलं दन्तनखभंगी रौक्षं च ॥ (सु.सू. 15/9)

According to acharya Sushrut in Asthi dhatu kshaya Pain in bones, dryness of skin, roughness and cracking of teeth and nails are the symptoms. In modern science this Asthi Dhatu Kshaya corelates to the symptoms of osteoporosis and osteopenia - which is due to loss of bone tissue because of deficiency of factors responsible for bone formation.

Asthi dhatu vriddhi

अध्यस्थिदन्तै दन्तास्थिभेदशूलं विवर्णता ।

केशलोमनखश्मश्रुदोषास्थिप्रकोपजाः ।। (च.सू. 28/16)

If there is Asthi Dhatu vriddhi there will be excessive and abnormal growth of bony tissue, extra teeth, discolouration, falling of hair, nail, beard, repeated fractures .

The modern science high bone density symptoms and signs are at par to the Asthi Dhatu vriddhi signs.

MAJJADHATU

करोति तत्र सौषिर्यमस्थनां मध्ये समीरणः ।

मदेसस्तानि पूर्यन्ते स्नेहो मज्जा ततः स्मृतः । (च.चि. 15 / 31)

Acharya charak says " that sameer (Vayu mahabhuta) creates space in bone which is filled by fatty substance.

महत्सु (अस्थिषु) च मज्जा भवति ।

स्थूलास्थिषु विशेषेण मज्जा त्वभ्यन्तराशितः । (सु.शा. 4 / 12,13)

In the inner part of long bones is present majja dhatu. If we try to understand this through Modern view point- According to Modern concept the long bones have Yellow bone marrow in it while Red bone marrow is present in small bones. Here this view of modern science is totally at par to ayurvedic theory. Ayurveda also recognises redbone marrow (Medo Dhatu) in small bones and yellow bone marrow (MajjaDhatu) in long bones.

Functions of Majja Dhatu

मज्जा प्रीतिं स्नेहं बलं शुक्रपुष्टिं पूरणमस्थां च करोति । (सु.सू. 15/5)

पूरणं (मज्जः श्रेष्ठं कर्म।) (अ.हृ.सू. 11/4)

The functions of Majja Dhatu according to acharya Sushrut is - Attachment, happiness, strength, shukra dhatu nourishment and filling up the Asthi Dhatu.

Majjakshaya

मज्ज्ञाक्षयेऽल्पशुक्रता पर्वभेदोऽस्थिनिस्तोदोऽस्थिशून्यता च ।

मज्जनि अस्थां सौषिर्य भ्रमस्तिमिरदर्शनम् ॥ (अ.हृ.सू. 11/19)

With depletion in quantity of Majja Dhatu there is emptiness within bones, vertigo, darkness according to ayurveda and the modern signs of decreased bone marrow symptoms too coincide with that of ayurvedic majja dhatu Kshaya symptoms.

Majja Dhatu Vriddhi

मज्जानेत्रांग गौरवम् ।

पर्वसु स्थूलमूलानि कुर्यात्कृच्छ्राण्यरूंषि च। (अ.हृ.सू. 11/11)

In Ashtangs Sangraha while explaining Majja Vriddhi features like "Rakta Gaurava" has been mentioned which indicates increase viscosity of blood in conditions where bone marrow is hyper proliferative e.g polycythemia of modern science.

Shukra Dhatu

(Reproductive tissue)

Its the last Dhatu -Saptam Dhatu of the Sapta Dhatu theory. Acharya charak says following shloka for Shukra dhatu

यथा मूकुलपुष्पस्य सुगंधो नोपलभ्यते ।लभ्यते तद्विकाशात्तु तथा शुक्रं हि देहिनाम् । (च.चि. 2 (4) / 39)

we can not smell the fragrance of a flower when it's budding but perceive the smell after it blossoms . Same is the case of Shukra dhatu, though it's always present in the body since birth but due to incomplete development of shukraveh srotas in childhood, it can not be assesed through its functions.

Since this Shukra Dhatu according to acharyas perform following functions in the body

"शुक्रादगर्भःप्रजायते (च.चि. 15/16)

"शुक्रधैर्यच्यवनेप्रीतिदेहबलंहर्षबीजार्थच(सु.सू 15/5)

Shukra Dhatu is the one which is responsible for the production of embryo / foetus which is due to sperm and ovum present in it. It's also the factor for courage, enthusiasm, love, affection and strength of the body. From the above shlokas we can conclude that Shukra Dhatu is the reproductive tissue of the body. Now lets turn to modern approach and knowledge of reproductive the leydig cells are well-nigh non existent in the testes during childhood when the testes secrete almost no testosterone although there number is quiet a lot Just as the shukra dhatu compared with an unblossomed bud who doesn't produce fragrance but the blossomed one does.

The presence of shukra Dhatu in the whole body is depicted by acharya charak under this Shloka

रस इक्ष्यौ यथा दध्नि सर्पिस्तैलं तिले यथा ।

सर्वत्रानुगतं देहे शुक्रं संस्पर्शने तथा। (च.चि. 2/(4)-46)

meaning there by that like the -Juice in sugar-cane, ghee in curd and oil in sesame seeds Shukra is present all over the body from the point of view of co-relation between shukra dhatu and its modern perspective it seems that the Shukra Dhatu represents androgens, semen and sperm, Gonadotrophic hormones. Since semen exists in whole and ejects out on sexual arousal. The mean sexual of arousal is tactile stimulation. According to Gangadhar the Shukra present in the twak (Tvaggatam Shukram) by continous erotic stimulation gets ejaculated. Sushruta explained the same phenomena for ejaculatory physiology and Lactation. Both are oozed out on tactile simulation

Concept of Shukra in stree

Ayurvedas concept of saptdhatu is irrespective of gender So, this shukra Dhatu is present in females as well Though Acharya Sushruta mentioned that if sexual activity happens in two sexually excited females there is secretion of Shukra - forming foetus without bones but Acharya Vaghbhatta clarifies and says that stree shukra is secreted during coitus and If we co-relate this with modern we will be more clear as this, fluid is nothing but the secretions of Bartholins, cervical and endometrial glands.

Now let us know the functions of shukra Dhatu.

Dhairya (courage):-

Dhairya means controlling power of mind, firmness, stability. A person devoid of it is likely to suffer from mental problems like depression, anxiety, stress etc. Acharya Dalhan described Dhairya as shoorta. This property of Shukra Dhatu is at par to the property of Testosterone. It's seen that females suffer from more anxiety, depression like disturbances during hormonal flux and are better if treated with testesterone therapy whereas such kindof disturbances are comparatively less apparent in men - owing to high testosterone levels in them.

Chyawan (ejaculation): -

Ayurveda describes eight factors for chyawan - that are harsha (excitement) tarsha (excesive desire) and sara(fluidity) pichilata (viscosity) gurutva(heaviness) anubhav (atomicity) Pravanabhava (tendency to flow out] Durt maruta [speedy motion of vata] chakaapani comments that due to pravanabhava shukra comes out where as sara, pichilta ,Gurutva etc are the physical properties of Shukra. According to modern - the degree of ejection is propotional to the degree of stimulation whether psychic or physical

PRITI [AFFECTION]

Acharya Dalhan described three phases of Priti

1. *Lust phase* - testosterone and estrogen secretions
2. *Attraction phase*- Adrenaline, dopamine, serotonin
3. *Attachment phase*- Vasopressin and oxytocin cause

long term bondings.phenylethylamine is the best Love chemical which is active in the early stages of relationships .oxcytocin is the Love Hormone which is released during physical contact

DEHBALA(Body strength)

Acharya Dathan describes dehbala as physical fitness. We pretty well know the role of testosterone and other androgens on the body musculature

HARSHA [sexual Desire)

Harsha is explained as the desire produced from Sankalp leading to erection and ejaculation. The glans have sensitive sensory end organs which send signals to spinal cord .These signals adjourn at levels of lower brain stem and thalamus the last order neurons adjourn at sensory cortex. This causes frequent sexual desire.

BIJARTH (Procreation)

Acharya sushrut regards the main function of shukra Dhatu as the production of progeny. The quantity of testosterone determines the fertility

5. MALA

Trimalas in Ayurveda
THE THREE TYPES OF BODY WASTES
www.rishioj.in
Purisha
Mutra
Sveda

Mala

मलिनीकरणान्मला:"

मृज्यते शोध्यते अनेतेति मलः

The ones that have property of polluting others are regarded as mala Ayurveda emphasises on Mala- i.e the waste matter of food is as important as the other body tissues for -maintenance of proper bodily functions. They bring about the purification of body by themselves getting expelled after a specific time and volume. Now the question that normally needs an answer is how come a thing thats a waste and has property of polluting others be considered as an important part of maintenance of health. It is said that

Shukrayattum balam pumsaam, malayattam tu jeevitam

which means the balance of semen provides strength to a person and the balance of excreta will guard one's life. In certain diseases like Rajayakshma (tuberculosis) the excreta is said to be bala i.e. strength to the body. It is said that in this disease protection of mala is line of treatment as whatever food we take is converted to faeces - and it becomes the source of nutrients and energy. On contrary to it in general the Mala which remains retained in the body from duration more than required it imparts pressure and causes blocks on the channels of transport in the body hampering the smooth functioning of the body, resulting in increase of making body seat of many diseases.

The mala maintains healthy state by their timely elimination. They keep the mind and senses pleasant and healthy. Example Of disturbed health and mind is commonly seen in people suffering from constipation or renal calculi.

Ayurved categorises these malas of two types

किट्टमन्नस्य विण्मूत्रं रसस्य तु कफोऽसृजः ।पित्तं मांसस्य खमलो मलः स्वेदस्तु मेदसः ॥

स्यात्किटं केशलोमास्थ्नो मज्जः स्नेहाक्षिविद् त्वचाम्। (च.चि. 15/18/

Aahar Mala

Dhatu Mala

Whatever be the type & mala all are Panchbhautiks in their constitution, all are required by the body and all are to be the excreted from the body eg urine is important for release of toxins from blood- but when "it's amount increases in body it has to be expelled out otherwise it will trigger many serious problems.

AAHAR MALA
AAHAR
[FOOD]
PURISHA
[FECUS]
MUTRA
[URINE]
SVEDA
[SWEAT]

Purisha(Faeces)

पक्वाशयं तु प्राप्तस्य शोष्यमाणस्य वह्निना । परिपिण्डितपक्वस्य वायुः स्यात्कटुभावतः । (च.चि. 15/11)

परिपिण्डितपक्वस्येति परिपिण्डितरूपतया मलरूपतया पक्वस्य। वायुः स्यात्कटुभावतः इति परिपिण्डितावस्थोद्भुत कटुता वायोरुत्पद्यते ॥(chakrapani for on Ch. Chi. 15/11)

The food material after digestion enters to pakwashaya where it is acted upon by agni and gets Converted into a semisolid consistency along with formation of Katu Vayu [Pungent] Now let's see what modern science has to say in this regard – it says that partially digested food passes from the small intestine to the large intestine or colon. within the colon digestion occurs by the action of bacterias. A large amount of gas, vitamin k and biotin are produced during the process and faeces are formed. In large intestine absorption of water and some electrolytes occurs which makes the undigested material hard and is called faeces.

Purish vegdharan

पक्वाशयशिरः शूलं वातवर्चोनिरोधनम् ।

पिण्डिकोद्वेष्टनाध्मानं पुरीषे स्याद्विधारिते ।। च० सू० 7/7

If for any reason purish tyag or mala tyag is not done, instead Vegdharan of adharniye vega is done it results in pain in intestine [abdomen] ,headache, Gas, pain in thigh muscles and bloating kind of symptoms precipitate according to acharya charak. In modern perspective if one avoids poop there can be severe abdominal discomfort or pain, bloating,faecal impaction,abdominal distention, rectal hyposensitivity, hemorrhoids and appendicitis etc are we can see by and large the symptoms are same in both the systems.

Mutra (urine)

Mutra mala is an essential metabolic waste product.

आहारस्य रसः सारः सारहीनो मलद्रवः ।

शिराभिस्तज्जलं नीतं वस्तौ मूत्रत्वमाप्नुयात् ।। शा० पू० 6/6

The essence g Aahar is Aahar Rasa which is responsible for supplying nutrition to all the dhatus and the wastage part of diet became mutra along with purisha. "

The liquid / fluid waste product is brought to basti [urinary bladder] by the the siras and its called mutra.

Functioning of urinary System

मत्राशयो मलाधारः प्राणायतनमत्तमम । से वह परीष पक्काशयगतास्तत्र नाडयो मत्रवहास्त याः ।। तर्पयन्ति सदा मत्रं सरितः सागरं यथा । सक्ष्मत्वान्नोपलभ्यन्ते मखान्यासां सहस्रशः ।। नाडीभिरुपनीतस्य मत्रस्यामाशयान्तरात । जाग्रतः स्वपतश्चैव स निःस्यन्देन पर्यते ।। आमखान्सलिले न्यस्तः पार्श्वभ्यः पर्यते नवः । घटो यथा तथा विद्धि वस्तिर्मूत्रेण पूर्यते ।। सु० नि० 3 /20, 23

Mutrashaya which is also Maladhara is a vital organ of the body. It is rich in siras (blood Vessels) and Snayus [Ligaments] in and around it. The vasti which continuously gets filled with mutra by mutravaha nadis and pores into vasti just as an earthen pot [with fine holes all around] dipped in water upto it's neck, gets water into it. Mutrashaya is very vital organ therefore it must have been kidneys according to sushrut and renal cortex is the amashya consisting of filtering units "the nephrons" and the pakwashaya in this context may mean major and minor calyx and nadis mean collecting tubules and medulla. The vasti may be considered as pelvis. Since even in modern system the pelvis is filled up continuously through the collecting tubules and calyx Just as water pores into an earthen pet from its sides.

Functions of mutra

बस्तिपूरणविक्लेदकृन्मूत्रम्" (सु.सू. 15/4)

The functions performed by mutra are:-

- It fills urinary bladder and keeps its functions intact.
- It is responsible for excretion of waste products.
- Helps maintain fluid balance.

- It keeps the body moistened.

The above mentioned functions of Mutra are in accordance with the functions of urinary system.

Symptoms of Mutrakshays.

मूत्रक्षये मूत्रकृच्छ्रं मूत्रवैवर्ण्यमेव च । पिपासा बाधते चास्य मुखं च परिशुष्यति ।।
च० सू० 17/70

When there is mutrakshaya there will be scanty urine, dark coloured urire, thirst dryness of mouth, pain in bladder .All these Symptoms and signs of Matrakshaya coincide with dysuria.

Mutra Vriddhi

मूत्रं मूत्रवृद्धिं मुहुर्मुहुः प्रवृत्तिं वस्तितोदमाध्मानं च ।सु० सू० 15/16

When there is increase in mutra quantity the Symptoms resemble that of polyuria, frequent urination, distension of bladder, repeated sensation to urinate.

SWEDA

It is one of the trinity of mala group

स्विद्यतेअनेनइतिस्वेद

meaning thereby the one responsible for production. of sweat [means vapour] is called sweda

यच्च (उदकम्) उष्मणानुबद्धं लोमकूपेभ्यः निष्पतत् स्वेदशब्दम् अवाप्नोति।

According to Charak Acharya the one situated near hair follicles in the skin and secretes watery secretions formed as sweat is termed as sweda. In ayurveda sweat is considered as sweda. In modern terminology sweat occurs through sweat glands present near the hair follicles on skin.

Functions of Sweda

स्वेदःक्लेदत्वक्सौकुमार्यकृत् (सु.सू. 1514)

- It keeps the skin and hair moist, smooth –
- It helps to maintain water balance in the body
- It excretes toxins from the body.

from modern point of view temperature regulation is the foremost function of sweat and in addition to it are the functions mentioned in Ayurveda.

Purisha(Faeces)

पक्वाशयेतुःप्राप्तस्यगोष्यमास्त्वहमलापरिपण्डितपस्वस्थायुःस्यात्तदुभावतः(ch.chi. 15/10)

The food material after digestion enters to pakwashaya where it is acted upon by agni and gets Converted into a semisolid consistency along with formation of Katu Vayu [Pungent] Now let's see what modern science has to say in this regard – it says that partially digested food passes from the small intestine to the large intestine or colon. within the colon digestion occurs by the action of bacterias. A large amount of gas, vitamin k and biotin are produced during the process and faeces are formed. In large intestine absorption of water and some electrolytes occurs which makes the undigested material hard and is called faeces.

Process of formation of purisha

Purishavaha srotas is the site of formation and excretion of purisha. Pakavashaya (large intestine) and sthula guda (anal canal) are the roots of purishvaha srotas.Purishdhara kala also called as "mala dhara kala ,plays vital role in formation of purisha.

According to modern cocept

Undigested food comes from ileum in to colon consist of indigestible material (cellulose) and liquid. Undigested food goes to colon water, salts, and vitamins are absorbed in to colon, and remaining content in the lumen becomes feces.

Characteristics of normal purisha

Characteritisics of normal purisha in terms of physical characteristics such as gandha (odor), varana (color), and vaishadya (unstickiness/clear) are not described separately in the ancient and medieval period texts of Ayurveda, but purisha pariksha has been given due to importance in context to diseases .Only pramana of purisha was described by Acharya charka as "sapta anjali" pramana.

Characteristics of normal stool

Color- light to dark brown due to presence of bile pigments

Odor-pungent smell which is caused by indole and skatole which are formed by bacterial fermentation and putrefaction.

Frequency-one to two per day and its painless

Consistency-In adult, the stool is well formed i.e, neither too hard nor too soft (about the consistency of a ripe banana)   Amount - Normal amount of feces in an adult is 100-200 g per day.

Purish pariksha is mentioned by yoga ratnakar under eight fold of examination. It is important as it has been given third place in asthavidh pariksha after nadi and mutra. Stool, contribute toward good health by getting eliminated in time. For the body to enjoy its health, it should be thrown out of the body in right proportions and in right time,

Importance of purisha pariksha

Status of agni (digestive fire)

Prognosis of disease

Symptoms of abnormal doshas

Presence of krimi

In patient of rajyasksma purisha is considered as "balam tasya hi vidbalam"

Importance of stool examination

Intestinal bleeding.

Infestation.

Inflammatory diseases.

Mal absorbtion.

To rule out Different causes of diarrhea

Purish vegdharan

पक्काशयशिरःशूलंवातरचनिरोधनम्पिण्डिकोद्वेष्टनाध्मानंपुरीषैस्याद्विध्यारिते (च.झू. 7/7)

If for any reason purish tyag or mala tyag is not done, instead Vegdharan of adharniye vega is done it results in pain in intestine [abdomen] ,headache, Gas, pain in thigh muscles and bloating kind of symptoms precipitate according to acharya charak. In modern perspective if one avoids poop there can be severe abdominal discomfort or pain, bloating,faecal impaction,abdominal distention, rectal hyposensitivity, hemorrhoids and appendicitis etc are we can see by and large the symptoms are same in both the systems.

Jala Nimajjana Purisha Pariksha (examination of stool by dipping in water)

This test determines the presence of Ama there by indicating state of digestive fire which is considered as major cause for different diseases. Test is based on the behavior of stools in water. If stool sinks in water, it indicates presence of Ama. If it floats, indicates, absence of Ama in stool. There are certain exceptions in which this test cannot be performed like if stool is too watery or too dry, very cold or vitiated by kapha

Examination of Feces

It can be divided in to three parts i.e, physical, chemical and microscopic examination.

Mutra (urine)

Mutra mala is an essential metabolic waste product.

आहारस्यरसःसारःसारहीनोमलद्रत : (शा-पू. 6/7)

The essence g Aahar is Aahar Rasa which is responsible for supplying nutrition to all the dhatus and the wastage part of diet became mutra along with purisha. "

शिराभिस्वज्जलंनीतबस्तौमूत्रत्वमाप्नुयात्" (शापू 6/7)

The fluid waste product is brought to basti [urinary bladder] by the the siras and its called mutra.Urine formation is one of the important physiologicalactivities of human body in which Mutravaha Moola and waste product of Aahar Rasa contributes significantly.Basti, Mutravaha Srotansi, Vrikka, Mutravaha Nadies, Mutravaha Dhamanis and Mutravaha Sira, etc. are major body parts which play significant role in the process of urine formation. While modern science described urinary bladder, nephrons, kidney, ureters and urethra, etc. vital parts of urine formations.

Functioning of urinary System

मूत्राशयोमलायार : -------बस्तिमूत्रेणपूर्यते(सु.नि. 3/20)

Mutrashaya which is also Maladhara is a vital organ of the body. It is rich in siras (blood Vessels) and Snayus [Ligaments] in and around it. The vasti which continuously gets filled with mutra by mutravaha nadis and pores into vasti just as an earthen pot [with fine holes all around] dipped in water upto it's neck, gets water into it. Mutrashaya is very vital organ therefore it must have been kidneys according to sushrut and renal cortex is the amashya consisting of filtering units "the nephrons" and the pakwashaya in this context may mean major and minor calyx and nadis mean collecting tubules and medulla. The vasti may be considered as pelvis. Since even in modern system the pelvis is filled up continuously through the collecting tubules and calyx Just as water pores into an earthen pet from its sides.

Role of various parts in urine formations

Vrikka

It mainly performs functions of urine formation & blood purification thus can be correlates with kidney as per

modern science. There are two Vrikka inside the body found in lumbar regions at abdominal wall in Koshtha.

The major process of urine formation and blood filtration take places in Vrikka thus it is considered as main organ

of urinary system.

Basti

It can be correlates with urinary bladder as per modern science and considered as one of Kosthangas amongst many inside the body. As per Susruta Basti surrounded with Nabhi, Kati, Mushka, Vakshanas, Shepha and Guda. It store and evacuate urine thus play important role in the process of urinary excretion.

Gavini

There are two Gavini inside the body found both side of Basti, they receive Mutra coming from Antras and circulate it through Mutrashaya.

Mutrapraseka

Mutrapraseka is considered as outlet of Basti, which differ in size in male and female. The size of Mutrapraseka in female is about two Angulas while in male it is twelve Angulas. The function of Mutrapraseka in male is to carries Mutra as well as Shukra and in female it carries Mutra. Mutrapraseka can be correlates with urethra on the basis of functional similarity.

Mutravaha Srotas (Nephrons)

Mutravaha Srotas performs functioning like microchannels which carry Mutra and considered as Nephrons of modern science. They originate from Basti while Susruta considered Medhra also as roots of Mutravaha Srotas.

Mutravaha Nadis

Mutravaha Nadis are found between of Pakvashaya and Basti and they perform function of Mutra Nishyandana and carry Mutra from Pakvashaya to Basti in normal conditions of relaxation.

Mutravaha Dhamanis

Adhogami Dhamani move downwards and transport Mutra and Purisha, they are total three types each of ten in number moving towards Mutrabasti to perform function of Dharana and Yapan of Mutra.

Mutravaha Siras

These are considered as veins of urinary system carrying Mutra to Basti since they opens in lateral side of Basti and helps in process of Nishyandana. Urine formation as per modern science Urine is considered as waste product of body containing urea, uric acid, water, salt and other waste products. The major process occurs inside the kidney in three major stages; Glomerular Filtration, Tubular Reabsorption and Tubular Secretion.

Glomerular Filtration

The process mainly occurs through glomerular capillaries in which blood filtered out to form urine. The high pressure of blood into these capillaries facilitates process of filtration. The protein and blood cells are retained while most of other materials coming with blood circulation reached to Bowman's capsule to form ultrafiltrate with the rate of 125ml/min.

Tubular Reabsorption

Some essential substances (potassium, sodium chloride, amino acids, bicarbonate and water) are reabsorbed at tubular part of nephrone through passive and active transport. The process of others co-transport also facilitate tubular reabsorption.

Tubular Secretion

Peritubular capillaries help to secret ions, substances which not flittered through glomerular filtration like some drugs secreted into the filtrate by process of tubular secretion. The ion exchange also facilitates process of tubular secretion. The nephron mainly involves in the formation of urine and each nephron is made by renal corpuscle and renal tubule. The renal corpuscle further divided into glomerular capillaries and Bowman's capsule, these organs mainly perform filtration of blood to from urinary fluid. Afferent arteriole brings blood into the glomerulus while efferent arteriole takes blood away from the glomerulus. The renal tubular parts also divided into various parts; Proximal Convoluted Tubule, Loop of Henle and Distal Convoluted

Tubule. The Proximal Convoluted Tubule reabsorbed substances, ions and water. Loop of Henle performs reabsorption and secretion of water while Distal Convoluted Tubule helps in restoration of ions and water.

Functions of mutra

बस्तिपूरणविक्लेदकृन्मूत्रम्" (सु.सू. 15/4)

The functions performed by mutra are:-

- It fills urinary bladder and keeps its functions intact.
- It is responsible for excretion of waste products.
- Helps maintain fluid balance.
- It keeps the body moistened.

The above mentioned functions of Mutra are in accordance with the functions of urinary system.

Symptoms of Mutrakshays.

मूत्रक्षयेमूत्रकृच्छंमूत्रर्णमेवचपिपासाबाधतेचास्यमुखेचपरिशुष्यति(च.सू.17/71)

When there is mutrakshaya there will be scanty urine, dark coloured urire, thirst dryness of mouth, pain in bladder .All these Symptoms and signs of Matrakshaya coincide with dysuria.

Mutra Vriddhi

मूत्रमूत्रवृद्धिमुहुर्मुहःप्रवृत्तिवस्तितोमाध्मानंच

When there is increase in mutra quantity the Symptoms resemble that of polyuria, frequent urination, distension of bladder, repeated sensation to urinate.

SWEDA

It is one of the trinity of mala group

स्विद्यतेअनेनइतिस्वेद

meaning thereby the one responsible for production. of sweat [means vapour] is called sweda

"यच्च (उदकम्) उष्मणानुबद्धलोमकूपेभ्यःनिष्पतत्स्वेदशब्दम्अवाप्नोति"

According to Charak Acharya the one situated near hair follicles in the skin and secretes watery secretions formed as sweat is termed as sweda. In ayurveda sweat is considered as sweda. In modern terminology sweat occurs through sweat glands present near the hair follicles.

Physiology of sweating and thermoregulation was well conceived by Ancient Ayurveda scholars. The detailed description of Svedavaha Srotas (channels carrying sweat), Sveda (sweat) as Mala (waste), its mechanism of formation on exposure to heat, therapeutic application of heat for inducing sweating under the concept of Svedan Karma (sudation) for purification and balancing the Dosha for management of disorders reflects the deep understanding of Ayurveda scholars about the physiology of sweating and temperature regulation.

Sweat is a fraction of Udaka (water) that comes out of Lomakoop (skin pores/hair follicles) on exposure to heat. Sweda has been considered as Mala of both Aahara and Meda Dhatu, as it is formed during digestion and metabolism. It has been also considered as Upa Dhatu of Meda Dhatu

Sweda is carried by Swedavaha Srotas

the Moola of Swedavaha Srotas is -Lomakoopa and Meda

Functions of Sweda

स्वेदःक्लेदत्वक्सौकुमार्यकृत् (सु.सू. 1514)

- It keeps the skin and hair moist, smooth –

- It helps to maintain water balance in the body
- It excretes toxins from the body.

from modern point of view temperature regulation is the foremost function of sweat and in addition to it are the functions mentioned in Ayurveda.

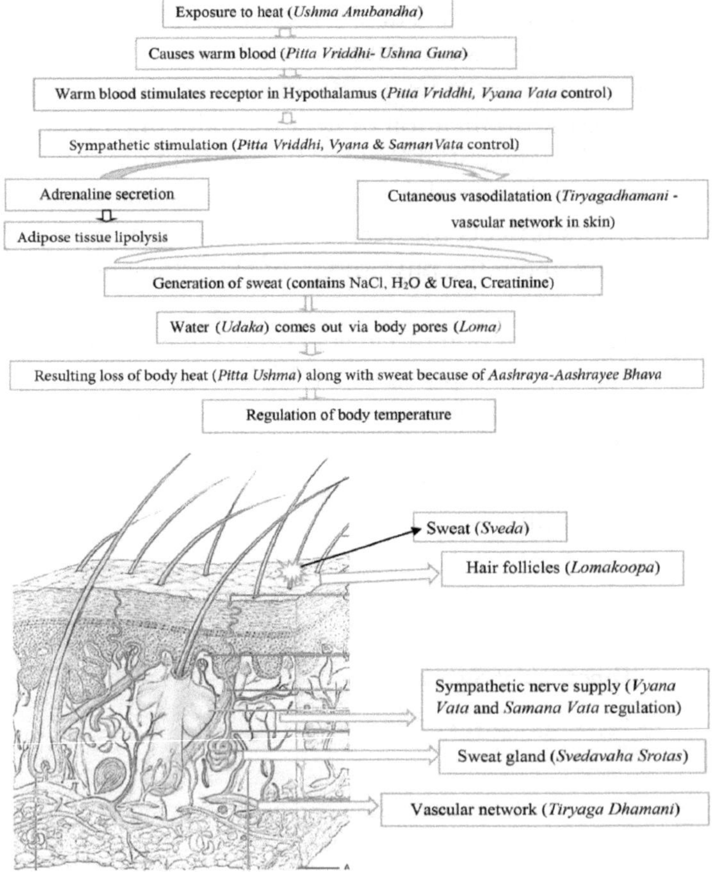

6. AGNI

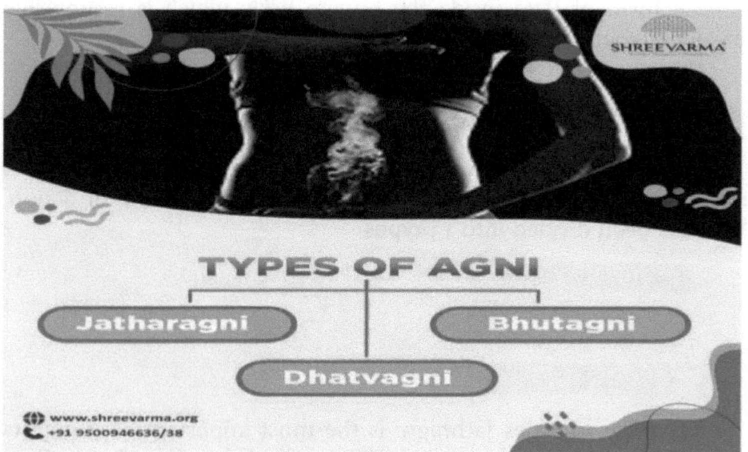

AGNI

निरुक्ति- *अङ्गति ऊर्ध्वंगच्छति इति। (निरुक्त)*

. Meaning - One which moves upward.

The concept of Agni is first encountered in the first veda, Rigveda'. Agni is described in Rigveda as a supernatural power, considered a deity. Ayurveda being an upaveda-sub-branch of the fourth veda 'Atharvaveda', also presents the Agni in deity form having a Godly nature. Agni produces enthusiastic energy for every activity

जाठरो भगवानग्निरीश्वरोऽन्नस्य पाचकः । सौक्ष्म्याद् रसानाददानो विवेक्तुं नेवशक्यते ॥ (सु.सू. 35/27)

Agni, with respect to health, is responsible for digestion and offers health to all.

Agni literally means fire in sanskrit, but in physio-chemical, biophysical and bio-chemical sequences this term does not actually mean fire

अंगतिव्याप्नोतिइतिअग्निः

That which is present in each and every cell .In Ayurveda the concept of Agni is implicit or directly linked up with the biological Agni in form of Pitta inside the human body which is responsible for all metabolic activities

अग्निरेवशरीरेपित्तान्तर्गतःकुपिताकुपितशुभाशुभानिकरोति (च.सू.17/1)

Agni is the invariable agent in the process of Paaka (digestion and transformation). According to the functions and site of action, Agni has been divided into 13 types

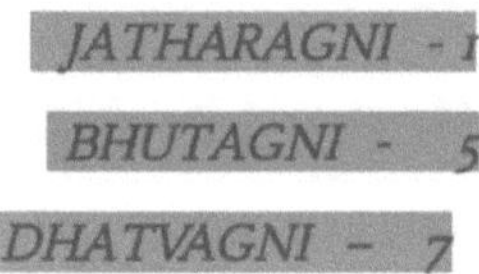

Of these 13 types Jathragni is the most important as it digests and transforms shadrasa and - Chaturvidh Aahar into Aahar Rasa and Mala. This Aahar Rasa is further worked upon by the relative bhutagnis of the mahabhuttas present in Aahar Rasa, which is later on worked by specific Dhatvagnis of Sapta dhtus.

जाठरः प्राणिनामग्निः काय इत्यभिधीयते। यस्तं चिकित्सेत सीदन्तं स वैकायचिकित्सकः।।

The treatment for abnormality of Agni to bring it back to normal functioning is the Kayachikitsa – Internal Medicine. . Almost all the diseases are created due to manda agni (manda meaning low). Protection of Agni is very essential in treatment of all diseases

Agni's subtle nature: सूक्ष्मत्वम्-This functional energy Agni cannot be physically put forth because of its subtle nature. Its presence is felt, reflected as a symptom but cannot be seen or presented as one particular object

Seat of Agni-Agni resides at the naval , Pittadhara Kala and Grahani are explained as places of Agni's existence. The seat of Agni is mentioned within the description of the organ Grahani (small intestine) , (Grahani is small intestine where main digestive juices are secreted from Liver and Pancreas having properties of the Pachaka pitta.)

Agni converts food in the form of energy. which is responsible for all the vital functions of our body. Therefore Dehagni is considered as the reason of life, complexion, strength, health, nourishment, lustre, oja, teja and prana. In Brahmsutra, Agni has been mentioned as sign of life. Yasaka shankaracharya illustrates that Agni carries everything in it. It burns, assimilates. Agni is a pivot around which the remaining factors responsible for the maintenance of health and causation of disease. as well as decay revolve. According to sushruta there is no agni in body but in the form of pitta. Acharya Bhoj also supports sushrut view.

JATHARAGNI

This is the bioenergy present in JATHAR [Stomach & Duodenum]. Ashtang hridya considers its seat in Grahni [Duodenum] where as Dhanvantari says its seat to be in Pittdhara kala " situated at the entrance of the Pakvashya [Intestine] and acting as a bolt to the door of the pathway/ channel of food. It is considered to be the one responsible for healthy life, strength to Dhatwagni and Bhutagni. This Jatharagni being the foremost of all other agnis in respect of its action it has to be in balance in order to maintain health.

Acharya charak divides this agni into four types according to the Dosha involved

Vishamagni **when the vata Dosha dominates**

Tikshanagni **when Pitta Dosha dominates**

Mandagni **Vata - Kapha dominates**

Samagni **when All Doshas in Balance**

VISHAMAGNI

There is an imbalance in digestion process. Sometimes its proper and sometimes improper or delayed.

TIKSHANAGNI

There is a Faster digestion process taking place owing to increased Pitta Dosha.

MANDAGNI

There is overall slowing down of digestion.

SAMAGNI :

When the food taken is digested and assimilated properly.

BHUTAGNI

Bhutagni is the agni of the five basic elements. Everything in this universe is composed of the five basic elements. These elements have their own five agnis or energies. Charak Says that these bhutagnis digest materials containing the elements and qualities similar to each bhutas Nourishes their own specific elements of the body.

In modern perspective the actions of jatharagni can be corelated to the digestion In Stomach and duodenum, and the action of the bhutagni can be equated with the conversion of digested materials in the liver.

DHATVAGNI :

All the seven dhatus [Bodily Tissues] contain their own smotas Rasag of Mam Bagni f Rasa Dhatu Raktagni % Rakta Dhatu Mames Dhatu, Medague of Meda Phatu, Asthyagri of Asthi Thalu, Majgagns of Majja hatu, Shukragni of Shukan Phatu. Each Dhatvagni or the bioenergy present in each Dhatu synthesiges and transforms the essential Aahar Rasa required for thep particular Dhatu This action is o selective action. that cort of regarding Pitta and agni.

The conclusion drawn, from the Various theories of acharyas is that for the sake of treatment Pitta and Agni are same though in build up they differ from each other. Agni is critically important to our over all well being. Agni works intelligently and cautiously on each and every cell of the body deciding and discriminating the substances with their transformation and digestion particularly and specifically for different cell types

Functions of agni

- - Digestion, absorption, assimilation
- Transformation
- metabolic activities Tissue nutrition
- fear, anxiety, anger.
- confusion, depression low energy, fatigue
- Sinus
- bloating constipation/diarrhoea
- hyperacidity, ulcers.
- production of Ojas, tejas, prana
- skin complexion, glow, Luster. maintainging body temperature mental alertness, clarity, reasoning, togic
- courage - confidence
- Patience, stability, Longevity However if this agni gets disturbed it can result in
- Emotional disturbances

So far whatever we have gone through the knowledge and understanding of AGINI It Seems totally justified why Ayurveda has emphasised so much on it why AGNI is rendered so much of importance since its the central power around which rest of the factors of wellness srevolve in all ayurvedic treatment parts be it for any underlying. disease the focus of every ayurvedist is to work on maintaining agni in equilibrium. According to acharys charak if there is no agni it indicates death. As all the bloenergy work, Dhatu functions and maintenance as well as mala formation excretion- think of any physiological action taking place - there is requirement of energy. in the form of AGNI .

In modern perspective ,agni is hydrochloric acid,all the digestive enzymes and hormones playing role in digestion ,absorption of ingested food along with the nourishment of bodily tissues.

7. PRAKRITI

PRAKRITI

Genes are the major reason for the prakriti, (Sanskrit: "nature," "source") in the Samkhya system (darshan) of Indian philosophy, material nature in its germinal state, eternal and beyond perception is uniqueness.

Genetics is the branch of biology and medical science which has much to reveal about the genetic background of an individual, its hereditary traits, DNA, and genetic variations. This field has much advanced researches to its crown. Everyday new theories and new informations are being added in this field of science. It helps to understand the uniqueness of each individual, uniqueness of family traits, uniqueness of race, uniqueness of country traits, uniqueness of enviromental traits etc . They are present in each cell of the body with a unique coding-helping and making each individual a unique identity and personality. Personality is one thing which every era people have been always interested to know about, be it of themselves , their loved ones or acquaintances. So much so that the age old Health system of Ayurveda had put a lot of light on the personality of an individual with respect to its physical and mental traits. *Prakritis* are discrete phenotypes and they are determined on the basis of physical, psychological, physiological and behavioural traits and interdependent of social, ethnic and geographical variables.

Since *Prakritis* underlie an individual's predisposition to disease as well as response to treatment, it is imperative in *Ayurvedic* practice to identify the *Prakriti* of a patient before treatment. A person's prakruti is the inherent balance of the three doshas at the moment of their creation. It is at this moment that a person's physiological and psychological tendencies become fixed.

To know a person's constitution is to know their tendencies. If a person knows their tendencies they can take the actions that keep their tendencies in check. A person who knows that they have a tendency to feel cold, easily avoids becoming too cold by wearing more clothing or drinking warm beverages. To know your constitutional tendencies is to be empowered with the knowledge needed to create balance in your life. Every living creature has all three doshas within them. We cannot exist without a certain amount of each. Kapha provides each of us with tissues, pitta provides metabolic action and vata allows us to move and express ourselves. Our constitution is best defined in terms of the percentage of each energy within a person's constitution.

In this way there are not three types (vata, pitta or kapha), or even seven types (combinations), but an infinite number of combinations and permutations with no two people being exactly the same. Regardless of a person's constitution, a person can have an imbalance in any dosha. Imbalances are created by the environment a person finds him or herself in and their lifestyle. For example; any person will become hot and vitiate pitta dosha if the temperature is hot enough. However, a person of pitta prakruti would become hot more quickly as they already have a tendency to feel hot. Thus, it can be said that a person with a pitta nature has a tendency toward a pitta imbalance. Likewise, everyone will vitiate their vata dosha if they find themselves moving about too much or too quickly. We live in a fast paced world. The pace of life today often causes vata imbalances regardless of the constitution of an individual. However, a person with a vata constitution will develop a vata imbalance more quickly than others. It does not take as much motion as it would for someone with a more stable (kapha) nature.

The prakriti of the patient is best determined by the most stable factors of a person's nature. The most stable factors reveal the deeper tendencies of a patient. The physical structure of a patient gives the greatest clue toward constitutional tendencies. While structure can change due to imbalances, it is the least likely to change, except for body weight. Hence, it is more reliable than functional indicators. Functional indicators, however, are still useful when they reveal lifelong patterns. Another good indicator of prakruti is the nature of the voice and the basic personality. While these can change, they usually do so only when a person is exposed to great trauma. Even then, they often will not change.

Functional indicators, such as patterns of digestion, elimination or sleep, can be used to assess both prakruti and vikruti. While patterns present over the course of one's life are indicators of prakruti, any tendency expressing itself right now is an indicator of vikruti.

Ayurveda, the Indian traditional system of medicine describes a unique concept "*prakriti*", genetically determined, categorising the population into several subgroups based on phenotypic characters like appearance, temperament and habits. The concept is claimed to be useful in predicting an individual's susceptibility to a particular disease, prognosis of that illness and selection of therapy.

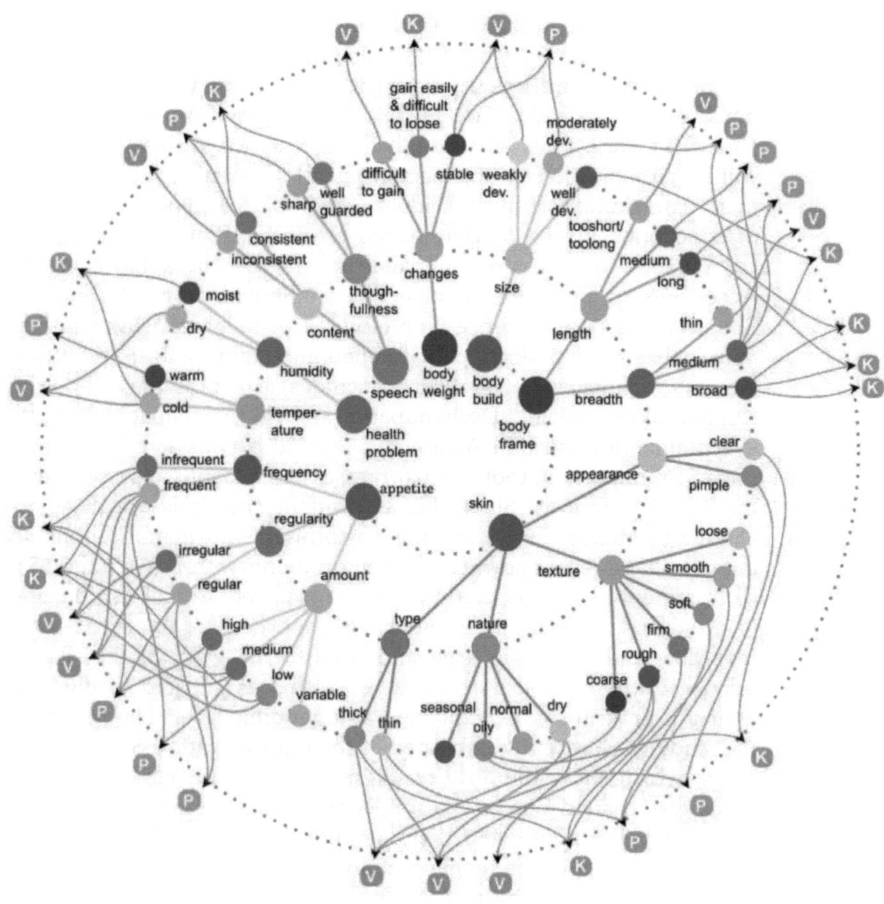

Ayurveda says

शुक्रशोणितसंयोगे यो भवेद्दोष उत्कटः । प्रकृतिर्जायते तेन तस्या में लक्षणं शृणु। (सु.शा. 4/63)

प्रकोपो वान्यभावो वा क्षयो वा नोपजायते । प्रकृतीनां स्वभावेन जायते तु गतायुषः । ।

सु० शा० 4/77

प्रकृतिस्वभावइतिउच्यते

All these above mentioned shlokas conclusion is that Prakriti word stands for natural. So whatever traits are inborn in an individual be it regarding the physical traits, mental behaviour, cognitions etc all the traits are unique in an individual these unique combinations in each individual are by birth and there is no scope of any change in these traits all through the life, if any change occurs it will be an indication of approaching death. Prakriti is the psychosomatic constitution of an individual which is determined at the time of conception by the predominance of Dosha. Prakriti is a unique combination by the predominance of all the three bio-energies. According to Sushrut the characters inherited from shukra and Shonit at the time of conception along with Kalgarbhashya prakriti, matrijaahar-vihar prakriti, panchmahabhut vikara, prakriti, the other factors influencing Prakriti includesJati prasahta Prakriti, Kulaprasakta prakriti, -Deshanupatini Prakriti ,kalanupatini Prakriti, -Vayonupatini prakriti.In Ayurveda , prakriti is considered as one of the most important tool used for assessing persons disease, treatment and prognosis. Since this assessment criteria is not a generalised one rather there comes a customised information about an individuals physical and mental strength along with other traits of it so treatment plans, diet plans, excercise plans etc will all also be customized and more result oriented. This approach of Ayurveda is remarkable and unique in itself and adds to the glory of the holistic science. Almost six years back a research was initiated to dig the querry if prakriti can be explained at a genomic level. The results of the study were recently published in the journal Nature Scientific reports, which show the answer might very well be Yes. An experiment was carried out on 3000 people with final cut of 262 with Ekdosha prakriti to assess their genome level. The DNA of these 262 was assessed. 52 genetic markers were found in only one dosha but not the others. A strong expression of the gene PGM1, which is responsible for sugar metabolism in the body was seen in Pitta Dosha Prakriti.

Many more studies and researches in this regard are still going on. The studies so far suggest that the phenotypic classification of India's traditional medicine has a clear genomic and epigenomic basis.

If we try to understand the genetic approach of modern science even at Literary level, we find that its the DNA of Genes which is responsible for uniqueness of an individual, which makes a person an individual Identity - different from others. In same pattern is Ayurvedas approach of prakriti The patterns of prakriti according to different Dosha combinations are further unique as the traits of the Dosha in a prakriti differs in different individuals and Stand's them unique and different from those sharing the Same Dosha combination.

Fundamental object of Ayurveda is not limited only to prevention and cure of the diseases but to provide bliss for complete happiness by maintaining total health called chaturvidha purushartha i.e. (Dharma(virtuous Acts)Artha((Possessing appropriately required wealth with judicious means)Kama (Gratification of Desires)Moksha(Emancipation/Salvation).Accordingly foundation of Ayurveda science is based on the ancient philosophy which are fundamental sciences of the ancient Indian think tank.

As Roga(Disease) is a great obstacle in attainment of these objects the science of Ayurveda is meant to provide assistance in the achievement of the basic goals by providing absolute health to all creatures on the earth in general and human in particular.

Fundamental concept of structural, functional and pharmacological branches of Ayurveda is based on metaphysical doctrine of *pancha-mahabhutas(five foundation blocks) which are the proto elements of universe & life.P*syche (soul/mind) concepts in Ayurveda is based on well established doctrine of *trigunas.B*esides this, the *pancha-mahabhutas* are the consequent evolutes of *trigunatmaka prakriti*(constitution). According to *Samkhya school(one of school of Indian phylosphy), prakriti* is the matrix of whole psycho-physical universe. It is the **equilibrium of *sattava, rajasa* and *tamasa(trigunas)* forms the ultimate ground for all existence.** When the equilibrium of *sattava, rajasa* and *tamasa* is disturbed under the influence of self, the process of creation starts, which is manifested in the form of *buddhi* (intellect), *ahamkara*(ego), *manasa*(mind), life and five eternal basic substances *Acharya Chakrapani a renowned commentator of Agnivesh samhita now famous as charak samhita understood* the philosophical concept of *prakriti* and *vikariti* which is evolved from previous sources in a bit different perspective.

Prakriti is the balance

The word *Prakriti*(constitution) has varying meanings in different contexts e.g. *samya*(equilibrium), *arogya*(health), *svabhav*(nature), *karana*, end stage of life, bodily constitution etc.

Physical constitution(Deha prakriti)

The present context of description of *Prakriti*(constitution) is in context to the body constitution i.e. *Deha Prakriti*(physical constitution). The approach of Ayurveda on the subject of *deha prakriti*(physical constitution) is quite detailed and vivid. Ancient schoalrs have enumerated a number of factors, which together lay the psychological and physical make up of an individual. The combination of these factors and the escalated state of *doshas* in *shukra* (sperm) and *artava* (ovum) at the time of conception determines the *Prakriti* (constitution) of a person. Though intensified *doshas* are capable of inducing destruction, but during formation of *prakriti*(constitution), there is '*Sahaja Satmya*' of *doshas*, which does not cause any harm to body. Hence constitution is emerged in balanced or *satmyaja* or *sahaja* increased state of *doshas*, although this increased status of *doshas* has superior and inferior effects on psyche and body, on the basis of which independent or mixed *prakriti*(constitution) gets matarialised.

Building blocks of life *vata, pitta, kapha, rasa, rakta,Mansa,Meda,Asthi,Majja,,Shukra and sattva,* rajas and tamas contribute as quantitative and qualitative indicators of health. Disequilibrium in these measures lead to dis-ease. Although absolute equilibrium of *dhatu*(basic tissues) is always not possible e.g. *kapha* invariably gets vitiated in the first part of the day and night, immediately after taking meals and in childhood, but a slight disturbance in the equilibrium of *dhatu*(basic tissues) does not cause any distinct uneasiness or *vikara,* hence in the case of natural disbalance of equilibrium of *dhatus*(basic tissues) does not cause any distinct uneasiness in the body and as such can be regarded as a normal condition.In other words equilibrium of *dhatus*(basic tissues) even includes conditions where there is minimal deviation from normalcy due to natural reasons.

Benefits of knowing prakriti

Ayurveda have put forth a strong foundation to make an understanding of human constitution. The *Ayurvedic* concept of *Prakriti* (constitution) is helpful in maintaining health, understanding disease and its management. Also, attainment of *Purusharth Chatushtaya* (Dharm-Artha-Kama-Mokha) which is only possible by an healthy individual.Knowledge of one's own *prakriti* (constitution) can be helpful in maintenance of one's health by following appropriate life style , diet and regimen suitable amental similarities in the mankind, dissimilitude from individual to individual is very common and natural. The factors responsible for these differences are multifarious and they together exert effect on constitutional, temperamental, psychological and spiritual make up of each individual.

Features	*Vata*	*Pitta*	*Kapha*
Body frame	Thin	Medium	Broad
Body build and musculature	Weakly developed	Moderate	Well-developed
Skin	Dry and cracked	Soft, thin, with tendency for moles, acne and freckles	Smooth and firm, complexion
Hair	Dry, thin, prone to breaks	Thin, oily, early greying	Thick, smooth, ar
Weight gain	Recalcitrant	Fluctuating	Tendency to obes
Food and bowel habits	Frequent, variable, and irregular	Higher capacity for food and water consumption	Low digestive ca and stable food h
Movements and physical activities	Excessive and brisk	Moderate	Less mobile and s
Tolerance for seasonal weather	Cold intolerant	Heat intolerant	Tolerant to both h and cold
Disease resistance and healing capacity	Poor	Good	Excellent
Metabolism of toxic substances	Moderate	Quick	Poor
Communication	Talkative	Sharp, incisive communication with analytical abilities	Less vocal with g communication s
Initiation capabilities	Quick, responsive, and enthusiastic	Moderate, upon conviction and understanding	Slow to initiate ne things
Memory	Quick at grasping but poor retention	Moderate grasping and retention	Slow grasping bu retention
Ageing	Fast	Moderate	Slow
Disease predisposition/poor prognosis	Developmental, neurological, dementia, movement and speech disorders, arrhythmias	Ulcer, bleeding disorders, skin diseases	Obesity, diabetes atherosclerotic co

Types of Prakriti(constitution)

Doshic Prakriti (Humoural constitution)

***Vata Prakriti*(constitution) *Heena*(Poor-weak)** *Panchbhautic* structure of *Vata* is *akasha* and *vayu* and its function is *rajasika* thus is concerned with the production of those somatic and psychic processes which are predominantly *rajasika* or dynamic in nature, hence the presence of *vata* is to be inferred in such mental phenomena as the exhibition of enthusiasm, concentration etc. It upholds all the supporting constituents and their due circulation throughout the body. Anomalous diet and regimen causing *vata dosha prakopa* results in *vata dosha* aggravation in *shukra*(sperm) and *shonita*(ovum). The aggravated *vata dosha* leads to the development of *fetus* of *vata prakriti*(constitution) which is depleted in physical and psychological qualities principally due to *apatarpana*(emaciating regimen) which leads to depletion in *dhatu*(basic tissues), as a consequence of which various inferior qualities are present in body and mind because of which *vata prakriti*(constitution) is deduced as heena

Pitta

***Prakriti*(constitution): *Madhyama*(medium,moderate)**- *Panchabhautic* structur of *pitta* is *tejasa*, its functions are *satvika* vision, digestion, heat-production, hunger, thirst softness, intelligence. Its presence is to be inferred in such mental phenomena as intellection and clear conception, as also such physical phenomenon as digestion, assimilation, heat-production, healthy appearance, courage, etc, ,Agni in body is provided by pitta This *agni* is inferred in body by digestion and metabolism. In the process of digestion of food, complex substances are broken down to simpler one and later on useful part and excretory parts are produced. Thus *agni* mainly causes process of catabolism. In balanced state of *pitta dosha* this process of catabolism is also in steady state equilibrium but if *pitta* remains increased, the process of catabolism of *dhatu* is more than their formation. As this *agni* is also predominant in brain, thus some good qualities related to intellect are found, but side by side anger, egoism, etc. are also present. Therefore *pitta prakriti*(constitution) is termed as *Madhyama* type.

Kapha

***Prakriti*(constitution): *Uttama*(strong)**- *Panchbhautic* structure of *kapha* is *apa* and *pithvi* (A.S.Su. 20), function is *tamas*, is concerned with the production of those physical and mental processes which are predominantly *tamasic* in nature i.e. conserving and stabilizing. Its presence to be inferred in such mental phenomena as the exhibition of courage, knowledge, understanding virility etc. and the physical phenomena as the production of bodily strength, build, integrities of structural elements of the body etc.Due to *kapha* predominance, *upachaya karma* (anabolic function) is predominant in the body, as a result of which body of *kapha prakriti*(constitution) *purusha* is firm, compact, plump. Muscles and joints are also well developed.*Kapha* is increased due to *santarpana*(diseases caused by over refreshing regimen) and therefore the person is not affected easily by *apatarpana*(diseases caused by emaciating therapies) vitiating *vata dosha*. Due to *sheeta*(coldness) and *snigdha*(unctuousness) qualities of *kapha*, *pitta vikara* do not influence easily. *Santarpanjanya vikara*(diseases caused by over refreshing regimen) are less as compared to *Aptarpanajanya vikara*(diseases caused by emaciating therapies). *Kaphaja purusha* has increased *tamasa* and *satva guna*. *Tamas guna* produces low grade qualities e.g. excessive sleep and *satva guna* produce many *sattvika* qualities e.g. calm and cool behaviour, excellent memory, dignity etc. Therefore, *kapha* *prakriti*(constitution) is considered *uttama*(best) among *doshaja prakriti*(constitution).

***Sama doshaja* or *Sama dhatu Prakriti* (Balanced constitution): *Shreshtha*(Ideal)** According to *Acharya Sushruta*, enhanced *vata, kapha* in their *prakrita* form result in development of *sama prakriti*(constitution). When single or mixed *dosha* predominance occurs, then superior and inferior both types of qualities are found in respective constitution. When predominant *tridosha* in their balanced (*prakrita*) form result in formation of *prakriti* (constitution), then only superior qualities of *doshas* are found. Hence *sama doshaja prakriti*(constitution) is *shreshtha* or best and rest are inferior

***Dvandaja Prakriti*(Dual humoural constitution): *Nindya* (denounced)** All three *dvandaja prakriti*(constitution) are said to be *nindya* (denounced).*Vata dosha* has *yogvahi guna*(catalytic property), then *vata pitta prakriti*(constitution) should be *madhyama*(medium) and *vata kapha prakriti*(constitution) should be *uttama*(best). Then why *dvandaja prakriti*(constitution) are labelled *nindaya* (denounced) . *Dvi-doshaja prakriti*(constitution) has *viruddha upkrama*5

***Sannipatika Prakriti* (Conglomerated humouralconstitution):** *Sannipatika prakriti*(constitution) results from abnormal predominance of *tridosha*.Most of the sages opine that abnormal predominance of *tridosha* can not result in formation of foetus.hence *sannipatika prakriti*(constitution) is not mentioned in *Brihat -trayi*. *Acharya Bhel* and *Harita* has mentioned this *Prakriti*(constitution) and considered it as worst (*jaghanya)* of all

Benefits of knowing Prakriti (Body constitution type)

- Personal analysis of Prakriti helps you know about your body and its requirements
- Knowing your Prakriti can help you maintain optimal health.
- It will help to maintain good and balanced personal, family and professional life
- Helps to plan lifestyle according to the requirements of body

- Prakriti analysis will help plan a balanced diet
- This can help to know likely occurrance of qualitative and quantitative imbalance in the body.

- **Vata .....kinetic energy....air+ether**

Pitta....thermal energy...fire+water

Kapha....potential energy...earth+water

Personality

Personality refers to individual differences in characteristic patterns of thinking, feeling and behaving. The study of personality focuses on two broad areas: One is understanding individual differences in particular personality characteristics, such as sociability or irritability. The other is understanding how the various parts of a person come together as a whole.**personality**, a characteristic way of thinking, feeling, and behaving. Personality embraces moods, attitudes, and opinions and is most clearly expressed in interactions with other people. It includes behavioral characteristics, both inherent and acquired, that distinguish one person from another and that can be observed in people's relations to the environment and to the social group.

This definition of personality and the reasons to assess it are in perfect co relation to ayurvedic concept of considering each individual as a unique identity.

Modern cocept of personality assessment is bascally divided into major four kinds of personalities

DOMNANCE

INFLUENCE

CONSCENTIOUSNESS

STEADINESS

Following features are categorised in each personality:-

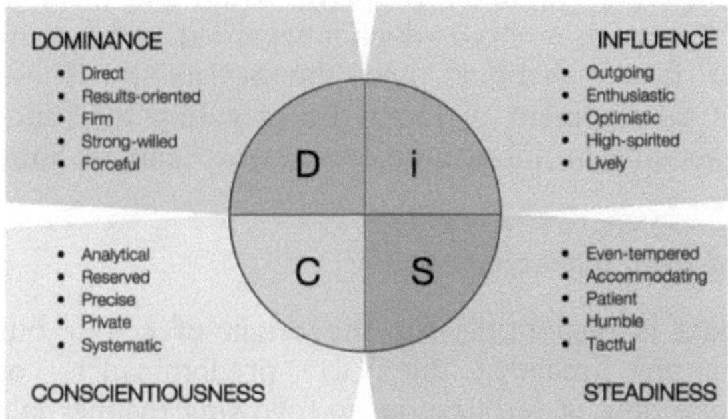

the features explained in modern perspective for various personalities are in accordance with the ayurvedic ways of prakriti analysis.

Sattvaja bhavas

Satava or different psychological endowment of the child is determined by psychological state of mother and father, behaviour of mother during pregnancy and purva janmakrita karma(Actions performed in previous life), strongely affects the following psychic nature of child more and these are:- Bhakti(likings), Moha(attachment), Gambheerya(seriousness), Bhaya(fear), Sheela desire not to partwith),mMriduta(softness), Tandra(drowsiness), Dvesha(animosity), Shourya(V

These factors are purely psychological traits. If we compare the atmaja bhava with the sattavaj bhavas, it is clear that in atmaja bhava most of those traits have already been included, which are fundamental to the expression of consciosousness.

Panchmahabhutas: Sukshma bhuta(subtle proto-elements) are derived from past actions and are associated with the sousness.

ul, along with mind/psych at the time of transmigration of soul from one body to other. Thus, sukshma(subtle) bhutas are linked with human organism from pre-embryonic period. Mahabhuta play a basic role in the constitution of shukra(sperm) and shonita(ovum) of father and mother and they are also the elementary constitution of the nourishing material.The union of sperm, ovum and the soul in the womb is designated as embryo which is regarded as the compound product of five mahabhuta and the atma(soul) These five bhuta instigate development of foetus by executing the functions of division, metabolism, lubrication, consistency and maturation in the embryo.

Factors, derived from mahabhutas

Tejas Mahabhuta is responsible for the origin of colour but variations in it are mainly due to predominance of one mahabhuta at the time of fertilization in following manner Jala mahabhuta is responsible for the creation of Gour varna Prithvi - Krishana varna, Prithvi+ Akash - Krishana shyam varna, Jala+ Akash - Gour shyam varna.

Accordingly it may be concluded that dominance of prticular mahabhuta affect development of human organism at sukshama(subtle) as well as sthula (Gross) levels. Independent narration of panvchabhoutik peakriti in shushruta samhita may be the the very base of this conceptwhile dealing with the constitution.

Matrija-Pitrija bhava (Hereditary factors):

Charaka samhita gives stress to the concept of hereditary transmission in depth and descrbes three micro fine constituents; bija, bijabhaga and bijabhagavayava of shukra and shonita. This may be accepted as sperm or ovum, chromosomes and genes respectively. Different organs develop from different parts of bija. Abnormality of the part of bija leads to deformity of the organ from that particular region of bija and its normalacy which develops in bijabhaga,foetus will be normal in otherwords if there is abnormality in bijabhaga concerned with development of artava and uterus, the foetus is supposed to be sterile. Thus it is acknowledged that different finer constituents for shukra(sperm) and shonita(ovum) (germoplasm) are responsible for the genetic or hereditary development. In modern fields of genetics it has been observed that all living things are a complex of a large number of independent heritable units. These genes are transferred to the offspring from the parents and the individual has his full complement of genes.

Pitrija Bhava(Paternal Source):

Kesha(hair of the head), Shmashru(hair of the face), Nakha(nail), Loma(small hair of the body), Danta(teeth), Asthi(bones), Sira(vessels), Snayu(muscles), Dhamni(arteries are inherited by paternal inheritance in an individual.

Matrija Bhava(maternal source)

Tvaka, Lohita, Mamsa, Medas, Nabhi, Hridaya, Kloma, Yakrita, pleeha, Basti, Vapavahanare inherited by maternal side.

Kala:

According to Acharyas different types of kala(time) can be interpreted as age of parents and time of copulation.

Time of copulation: Copulation is indicated only in anindaya kala(unforbidden) for attainment of a child of healthy state. The anindaya kala(unforbidden time) is, all the days of month except first four days of menstrual cycle, amavasya(The day of new moon), purnamasi(the day of full moon), Chaturdashi(the fourteenth day in a lunar half month), Ashtami (The eighth day in a lunar half month), Tryodashi. If copulation is done in nindaya kala(forbidden period), resulting child suffers from abnormalities of intelligence, strength and eyes

Garbhashaya(Uterus)

Stipulation of healthy uterus can be appraised from the fact that defective uterine condition along with other causes delays the conception even in fertile woman and if conception takes place, it will result in malformed child with respect to shape, colour and senses.

Matura ahara vihara(Marernal diet and regimen):

In Ayurveda, specific diet and activities have been introduced to obtain child of desired sex, colour, constitution e.g., woman aspiring for a son of tall, robust personality, fair complexion, resembling lion (in courage), energetic, chaste, endowed with qualities of goodness (satvika), is advised to follow the diet and activities as designated

Rasaja bhava(Nutritional factor):

Rasa is one of the important procreative factor for the heathy progeny. Here rasa stands for that very fluid of the mother by which the foetus is nourished and this very factor has been recognized as one of the determinants for the development of foetus/ neonate. Mother's diet contains all the rasas(tastes), thus the rasa(nutritive fluid) derived from this diet gives strength and complexion to the fetus, and the foetus deriving its sustenance from this rasa remains alive and develops in the uterus .Rasaja bhavaAbhirnirvritti of Sharira Abhivriddhi Tripti Sharira upachayaSthiti Prananubandha Bala(strength) Pushti Varna Utsaha Hani

Post natal factors:

Satmyaja Bhava(Congenious factor):

Satmya is elucidated as use of regimen and diet which is congruous with the body. Importance of satmyaja bhava(factor) can be ascertained from the fact that if asatmya things are not taken, then couples do not become infertile and also fetus is not defective. This factor thus has imptance in preconception,prenatal and post natal phase of the mother especially. Following are the satmya factors mentioned by Acharya .Arogya, Analasya, Alolupa (freedom from diseases, laziness and greed) *Svara (excellence of voice),Varna, Medha, Indriya prasada(clarity of senses), Ojas, Ayu(life), Bala(strength). Vayo-anupatini(According to age): Acharya Charaka enumerated kala(time) as a factor which is responsible for formation of difference in constitution and nature of an individual Kala is the sharira vriddhikara bhava(factor responsible for the growth of the body)) and bala vridhikar bhava(factors responsible for promotion of strength) i.e. proper development of body and vigor depends on kala(time)

Vaya (Age):

Vaya(Age) is defined as the state of sharira(body) which specially depends upon kala pramana(the length of time that has passed since birth) Vaya(Age) is divided into three categories as bala(young age), madhya(middle age) and jeerna(old age)

Balyavastha(young age}In the initial stage of balyavastha(young age), the body tissues are not mature and the signs of adolescence are not manifested. The person is delicate, intolerant to troubles, incomplete in strength and mainly kapha dosha is predominant. In the later stage of Balyavastha(young age) the person has generally undetermined psychic disposition.

Madhyavastha(middle age): In this stage man attains the balance of strength, energy, understanding, retention power, memory, speech and the person is of strong and well determined psychic disposition. There is predominance of pitta dosha.

Jeernavastha(old age): In this stage the body tissues, sense organs, strength, energy, understanding, retention capabilities, speech and discrimination begins to decay. The elements of body disintegrate; gradual wearing of body till the age of hundred years takes place. Vata dosha becomes predominant in this stage of life

Types of Prakriti(constitution)

Doshic Prakriti (Humoural constitution)

Vata Prakriti(constitution) Heena(Poor-weak) Panchbhautic structure of Vata is akasha and vayu and its function is rajasika thus is concerned with the production of those somatic and psychic processes which are predominantly rajasika or dynamic in nature, hence the presence of vata is to be inferred in such mental phenomena as the exhibition of enthusiasm, concentration etc. It upholds all the supporting constituents and their due circulation throughout the body. Anomalous diet and regimen causing vata dosha prakopa results in vata dosha aggravation in shukra(sperm) and shonita(ovum). The aggravated vata dosha leads to the development of fetus of vata prakriti(constitution) which is depleted in physical and psychological qualities principally due to apatarpana(emaciating regimen) which leads to depletion in dhatu(basic tissues), as a consequence of which various inferior qualities are present in body and mind because of which vata prakriti(constitution) is deduced as heena

Pitta Prakriti(constitution): Madhyama(medium,moderate)- Panchabhautic structure of pitta is tejasa, its functions are satvika vision, digestion, heat-production, hunger, thirst softness, intelligence. Its presence is to be inferred in such mental phenomena as intellection and clear conception, as also such physical phenomenon as digestion, assimilation, heat-production, healthy appearance, courage, etc, ,Agni in body is provided by pitta This agni is inferred in body by digestion and metabolism. In the process of digestion of food, complex substances are broken down to simpler one and later on useful part and excretory parts are produced. Thus agni mainly causes process of catabolism. In balanced state of pitta dosha this process of catabolism is also in steady state equilibrium but if pitta remains increased, the process of catabolism of dhatu is more than their formation. As this agni is also predominant in brain, thus some good qualities related to intellect are found, but side by side anger, egoism, etc. are also present. Therefore pitta prakriti(constitution) is termed as Madhyama type.

Kapha Prakriti(constitution): Uttama(strong)- Panchbhautic structure of kapha is apa and pithvi (A.S.Su. 20), function is tamas, is concerned with the production of those physical and mental processes which are predominantly tamasic in nature i.e. conserving and stabilizing. Its presence to be inferred in such mental phenomena as the exhibition of courage, knowledge, understanding virility etc. and the physical phenomena as the production of bodily strength, build, integrities of structural elements of the body etc.Due to kapha predominance, upachaya karma (anabolic function) is predominant in the body, as a result of which body of kapha prakriti(constitution) purusha is firm, compact, plump. Muscles and joints are also well developed.Kapha is increased due to santarpana(diseases caused by over refreshing regimen) and therefore the person is not affected easily by apatarpana(diseases caused by emaciating therapies) vitiating vata dosha. Due to sheeta(coldness) and snigdha(unctuousness) qualities of kapha, pitta vikara do not influence easily. Santarpanjanya vikara(diseases caused by over refreshing regimen) are less as compared to Aptarpanajanya vikara(diseases caused by emaciating therapies). Kaphaja purusha has increased tamasa and satva guna. Tamas guna produces low grade qualities e.g. excessive sleep and satva guna produce many sattvika qualities e.g. calm and cool behaviour, excellent memory, dignity etc. Therefore, kapha prakriti(constitution) is considered uttama(best) among doshaja prakriti(constitution).

Sama doshaja or Sama dhatu Prakriti (Balanced constitution): Shreshtha(Ideal) According to Acharya Sushruta, enhanced vata, kapha in their prakrita form result in development of sama prakriti(constitution). When single or mixed dosha predominance occurs, then superior and inferior both types of qualities are found in respective constitution. When predominant tridosha in their balanced (prakrita) form result in formation of prakriti (constitution), then only superior qualities of doshas are found. Hence sama doshaja prakriti(constitution) is shreshtha or best and rest are inferior

Dvandaja Prakriti(Dual humoural constitution): Nindya (denounced) All three dvandaja prakriti(constitution) are said to be nindya (denounced).Vata dosha has yogvahi guna(catalytic property), then vata pitta prakriti(constitution) should be madhyama(medium) and vata kapha prakriti(constitution) should be uttama(best). Then why dvandaja prakriti(constitution) are labelled nindaya (denounced) . Dvi-doshaja prakriti(constitution) has viruddha upkrama5

Sannipatika Prakriti (Conglomerated humouralconstitution): Sannipatika prakriti(constitution) results from abnormal predominance of tridosha.Most of the sages opine that abnormal predominance of tridosha can not result in formation of foetus.hence sannipatika prakriti(constitution) is not mentioned in Brihat -trayi. Acharya Bhel and Harita has mentioned this Prakriti(constitution) and considered it as worst (jaghanya) of all

Features	*Vata*	*Pitta*	*Kapha*
Body frame	Thin	Medium	Broad
Body build and musculature	Weakly developed	Moderate	Well-developed
Skin	Dry and cracked	Soft, thin, with tendency for moles, acne and freckles	Smooth and firm complexion
Hair	Dry, thin, prone to breaks	Thin, oily, early greying	Thick, smooth, a
Weight gain	Recalcitrant	Fluctuating	Tendency to obe
Food and bowel habits	Frequent, variable, and irregular	Higher capacity for food and water consumption	Low digestive ca and stable food h
Movements and physical activities	Excessive and brisk	Moderate	Less mobile and
Tolerance for seasonal weather	Cold intolerant	Heat intolerant	Tolerant to both and cold
Disease resistance and healing capacity	Poor	Good	Excellent
Metabolism of toxic substances	Moderate	Quick	Poor
Communication	Talkative	Sharp, incisive communication with analytical abilities	Less vocal with g communication s
Initiation capabilities	Quick, responsive, and enthusiastic	Moderate, upon conviction and understanding	Slow to initiate n things
Memory	Quick at grasping but poor retention	Moderate grasping and retention	Slow grasping bu retention
Ageing	Fast	Moderate	Slow
Disease predisposition/poor prognosis	Developmental, neurological, dementia, movement and speech disorders, arrhythmias	Ulcer, bleeding disorders, skin diseases	Obesity, diabete atherosclerotic c

Types of Prakriti(constitution)

Doshic Prakriti (Humoural constitution)

Vata Prakriti(constitution) Heena(Poor-weak) Panchbhautic structure of Vata is akasha and vayu and its function is rajasika thus is concerned with the production of those somatic and psychic processes which are predominantly rajasika or dynamic in nature, hence the presence of vata is to be inferred in such mental phenomena as the exhibition of enthusiasm, concentration etc. It upholds all the supporting constituents and their due circulation throughout the body. Anomalous diet and regimen causing vata dosha prakopa results in vata dosha aggravation in shukra(sperm) and shonita(ovum). The aggravated vata dosha leads to the development of fetus of vata prakriti(constitution) which is depleted in physical and psychological qualities principally due to apatarpana(emaciating regimen) which leads to depletion in dhatu(basic tissues), as a consequence of which various inferior qualities are present in body and mind because of which vata prakriti(constitution) is deduced as heena

Pitta Prakriti(constitution): Madhyama(medium,moderate)- Panchabhautic structure of pitta is tejasa, its functions are satvika vision, digestion, heat-production, hunger, thirst softness, intelligence. Its presence is to be inferred in such mental phenomena as intellection and clear conception, as also such physical phenomenon as digestion, assimilation, heat-production, healthy appearance, courage, etc, ,Agni in body is provided by pitta This agni is inferred in body by digestion and metabolism. In the process of digestion of food, complex substances are broken down to simpler one and later on useful part and excretory parts are produced. Thus agni mainly causes process of catabolism. In balanced state of pitta dosha this process of catabolism is also in steady state equilibrium but if pitta remains increased, the process of catabolism of dhatu is more than their formation. As this agni is also predominant in brain, thus some good qualities related to intellect are found, but side by side anger, egoism, etc. are also present. Therefore pitta prakriti(constitution) is termed as Madhyama type.

Kapha

Prakriti(constitution): Uttama(strong)- Panchbhautic structure of kapha is apa and pithvi (A.S.Su. 20), function is tamas, is concerned with the production of those physical and mental processes which are predominantly tamasic in nature i.e. conserving and stabilizing. Its presence to be inferred in such mental phenomena as the exhibition of courage, knowledge, understanding virility etc. and the physical phenomena as the production of bodily strength, build, integrities of structural elements of the body etc.Due to kapha predominance, upachaya karma (anabolic function) is predominant in the body, as a result of which body of kapha prakriti(constitution) purusha is firm, compact, plump. Muscles and joints are also well developed.Kapha is increased due to santarpana(diseases caused by over refreshing regimen) and therefore the person is not affected easily by apatarpana(diseases caused by emaciating therapies) vitiating vata dosha. Due to sheeta(coldness) and snigdha(unctuousness) qualities of kapha, pitta vikara do not influence easily. Santarpanjanya vikara(diseases caused by over refreshing regimen) are less as compared to Aptarpanajanya vikara(diseases caused by emaciating therapies). Kaphaja purusha has increased tamasa and satva guna. Tamas guna produces low grade qualities e.g. excessive sleep and satva guna produce many sattvika qualities e.g. calm and cool behaviour, excellent memory, dignity etc. Therefore, kapha prakriti(constitution) is considered uttama(best) among doshaja prakriti(constitution).

Sama doshaja or Sama dhatu Prakriti (Balanced constitution): Shreshtha(Ideal) According to Acharya Sushruta, enhanced vata, kapha in their prakrita form result in development of sama prakriti(constitution). When single or mixed dosha predominance occurs, then superior and inferior both types of qualities are found in respective constitution. When predominant tridosha in their balanced (prakrita) form result in formation of prakriti (constitution), then only superior qualities of doshas are found. Hence sama doshaja prakriti(constitution) is shreshtha or best and rest are inferior

Dvandaja Prakriti(Dual humoural constitution): Nindya (denounced) All three dvandaja prakriti(constitution) are said to be nindya (denounced).Vata dosha has yogvahi guna(catalytic property), then vata pitta prakriti(constitution) should be madhyama(medium) and vata kapha prakriti(constitution) should be uttama(best). Then why dvandaja prakriti(constitution) are labelled nindaya (denounced) . Dvi-doshaja prakriti(constitution) has viruddha upkrama5

Sannipatika Prakriti (Conglomerated humouralconstitution): Sannipatika prakriti(constitution) results from abnormal predominance of tridosha.Most of the sages opine that abnormal predominance of tridosha can not result in formation of foetus.hence sannipatika prakriti(constitution) is not mentioned in Brihat -trayi. Acharya Bhel and Harita has mentioned this Prakriti(constitution) and considered it as worst (jaghanya) of all

Benefits of knowing Prakriti (Body constitution type)

- Personal analysis of Prakriti helps you know about your body and its requirements
- Knowing your Prakriti can help you maintain optimal health.
- It will help to maintain good and balanced personal, family and professional life
- Helps to plan lifestyle according to the requirements of body
- Prakriti analysis will help plan a balanced diet
- This can help to know likely occurrance of qualitative and quantitative imbalance in the body.

- Vata .....kinetic energy....air+ether

Pitta....thermal energy...fire+water

Kapha....potential energy...earth+water

Personality

Personality refers to individual differences in characteristic patterns of thinking, feeling and behaving. The study of personality focuses on two broad areas: One is understanding individual differences in particular personality characteristics, such as sociability or irritability. The other is understanding how the various parts of a person come together as a whole.personality, a characteristic way of thinking, feeling, and behaving. Personality embraces moods, attitudes, and opinions and is most clearly expressed in interactions with other people. It includes behavioral characteristics, both inherent and acquired, that distinguish one person from another and that can be observed in people's relations to the environment and to the social group.

This definition of personality and the reasons to assess it are in perfect co relation to ayurvedic concept of considering each individual as a unique identity.

Modern cocept of personality assessment is bascally divided into major four kinds of personalities

DOMNANCE

INFLUENCE

CONSCENTIOUSNESS

STEADINESS

Following features are categorised in each personality:-

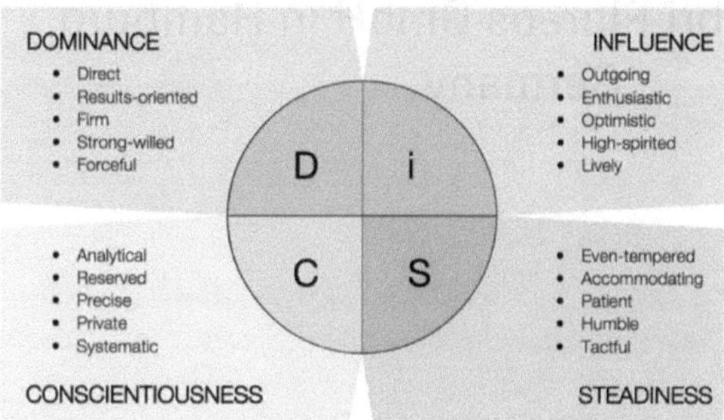

the features explained in modern perspective for various personalities are in accordance with the ayurvedic ways of prakriti analysis.

Printed by Libri Plureos GmbH in Hamburg,
Germany